MOUSE MORRIS

*His
Extraordinary
Racing Life*

MOUSE MORRIS

His Extraordinary Racing Life

Declan Colley

The Collins Press

PUBLISHED IN 2008 BY
The Collins Press
West Link Park
Doughcloyne
Wilton
Cork

British Library Cataloguing in Publication Data

Colley, Declan
Mouse Morris : the authorised biography
1. Morris, Michael 2. Racehorse trainers – Ireland –
Biography 3. Jockeys – Ireland – Biography
I. Title
798.4'0092
ISBN-13: 9781905172856

Typesetting by The Collins Press
Typeset in Bembo 12 pt
Printed in Malta by Gutenberg Press Ltd

Contents

For Máiréad, without whose endless encouragement, patience, assistance and belief, this book would never have happened at all.

Acknowledgements

Writing this book would have been impossible without the great help and assistance of the subject. Although initially a little dubious about having a book written about himself ('I'm way too young for that'), once the project was under way, Mouse was unfailingly helpful and surprisingly willing to discuss subjects which were often as painful to him as they were pertinent to the story. Without that help there would have been no book.

My thanks too must go to each and every one of those people I interviewed during the course of my research – those people who gave of their time with a willingness and enthusiasm which was certainly a welcome surprise to a cynical hack like myself. That willingness and enthusiasm most certainly reflects their collective fondness for Mouse Morris – the man and the horse trainer.

Others I must thank include Tom Murphy, Tim Vaughan and Tony Leen, respectively the Chief Executive, Editor and Sports Editor of the *Irish Examiner* who allowed me the time to undertake the project and whose support has been invaluable. Other *Examiner* personnel who must be thanked include Ireland's best racing writer, Pat Keane, as well as Tom Ahern, Alfie Hanrahan, Bob Lester, Colm O'Connor, Michael Moynihan and Larry Kavanagh.

The library staff in the *Examiner* must also be thanked, including Anne, Pat, Declan, Paul and the late Susan. Thanks, too, to Pam Mosier of the Carolina Cup Racing Association who was a huge help with the opening chapter.

Others whose enthusiasm and interest was unflagging include long-time Mouse supporter and adviser Martin Sheehan (who must bear some of the responsibility, as he helped shape the idea), all the boys (and gals) in the Briar Rose, including Ken, Murf, Cola, Burkey, Junior, Fred, Barry, Ross, Dan, Mac, Jackie and Orla, whose collective enthusiasm never wavered – even when mine did.

Much of the book was written in the tiny hamlet of Crookhaven in west Cork during the winter of 2007–8 and my gratitude must go to those local people who made life so much easier during that period, including Dermot and Alison O'Sullivan, Kevin Lynch and Tess Laycock, Angelique Power, Thomas Notter, Sonny and Denis O'Driscoll, Billy and Angela O'Sullivan, and Ann, Gerry, Willie and Jimmy O'Mahoney, as well as Rose and Colin, Heather and Hubert, Gavin, Charlie, Emma, Jack, Joey, Frank, Dave, Ciara, Lana and Seanie. Dolly the dog was also a constant companion throughout.

Aidan Power must also come in for special thanks not least for his unerring support, but also his invaluable help with the chapter on Lord Killanin and with the index.

My appreciation too must go to the staff at The Collins Press, as well as Cathy Thompson whose editing was as incisive and professional as it was painless.

Peter Mooney and Pat and Liam Healy were fantastic on the photographic front in coming up with the majority of the images in the book, as were Mouse's twin, John, and his wife Thelma, as well as Mouse himself, who would probably make a fine snapper if he were ever to give up the day job.

Great support also came from my brothers Austin and Mick, brother-in-law Eamonn, as well as lifetime friends Mark and Carol Phelan, Paul Doolin and Elizabeth Doran.

The two most senior women in my life, my mum Eithne and my mum-in-law May were also incredibly enthusiastic and I know that this book is as much of a dream come true for them as it is for me.

Finally, my dad, Michael, is sadly no longer with us, but I know he is smiling now that this project is completed. His vision ultimately made this possible and I'm just sad he's not here to see it.

Introduction

There's a small, dishevelled guy in the corner of Brid Hughes' bar in Spiddal. He's got a glass of Smithwicks in front of him and a bodhran in his hand. There's a pack of Major on the table and a bystander asks if he can have one.

'Mac an Lord, can I bum a fag?'

'Work away,' comes the response.

Alec Finn is there, Frankie Gavin is there; a whole gamut of Irish musical talent is there. The pub itself is heaving, the crowd anxiously anticipating the 'session' which is set to kick-off.

Hughes' Bar is the musical focal point of the village and notable as the birthplace of the band De Dannan, of which Finn and Gavin were founder members.

The small, dishevelled guy in the corner has been around these parts for many years. He's not a musician in the professional sense, but he has played bodhran in sessions such as these for almost as long as he can remember, usually with the crème de la crème of the Irish traditional scene.

He knows the likes of Paddy Moloney of The Chieftans and has jammed with those Irish music legends on many occasions in venues up and down the country. He's friends too with such as Dolores Keane, Eleanor Shanly, Ringo McDonagh and Jackie Daly – all of whom have had links with De Dannan down the years. He's at home here.

Although he no longer lives in Spiddal, he was born there and has undying bonds with the area – to the point, like his father before him, that his cars always carry a County Galway registration plate. He has a sense of being here in the heart of the Connemara gaeltacht and he positively comes alive on nights like these, when the music joyously washes over the appreciative audience.

'Mac an Lord,' they call him in these parts and there are not too many Irishmen who can pride themselves on such a nickname. But he is proud: proud of his heritage, proud of his background and proud of his Irishness.

His is an unusual Irish story in that his father was a real-life Lord whose ancestry can be traced back centuries, and the fact that the locals around these parts still affectionately embrace his children is not only a measure of the man himself, but also his offspring.

Those children have each gone their own ways – one is a film producer, another a photographer and falconer, one is an art therapist and yet another a jockey and horse trainer – but they still gravitate back to Spiddal as often as they can, as if to refuel emotionally and spiritually.

The small, dishevelled guy in the corner with the bodhran and the glass of Smithwicks and a packet of Major in front of him is one of those children and he is refuelling, drinking in the glory and unashamed joy of the moment.

He's a famous horse trainer now, although he does not necessarily fit the clichéd stereotype most people would associate with such a job. Although he has trained horses for most of Ireland's financial king pins down the years, he still doesn't endure type-casting.

His craggy features and his long unkempt hair are one thing; his singular – almost defiant – approach to his profession, which was at times financially treacherous, quite another. But, on the basis of his many successes down the years, his record is unconditionally laudable.

He is as at home here as he is overseeing work on his remarkable gallops in Tipperary; but this is leisure, the rest is work.

Around here he is simply 'Mac an Lord' – the Lord's son – but everywhere else he goes, he's known as Mouse Morris and his story bears telling.

1   The End and the Beginning

It was a clear but chilly November day at Camden in South Carolina – far removed from his normal milieu on the other side of the Atlantic – when Mouse Morris suffered a crashing fall during the eighth running of the Colonial Cup in 1977. The accident was to be a crucial turning point in the career of a man for whom riding racehorses had been the centre of his existence, since the resulting badly broken leg was to change his life forever – but at that stage he could never have imagined the sea-change which lay ahead.

It would take a long and painful recuperation period for the leg to mend and, even when it did heal, the Irishman was left to ponder medical prognoses that indicated his life as a jockey was certainly over. So stubborn and obstinate was he that he would ignore the doctors' pleadings for a further two years after the Colonial Cup disaster, until, as he now admits, he did not leave his life as a jockey: it left him.

As with many endings, Mouse Morris' departure from the life he loved so much and which had brought him such success was painful and bitter. He had been rendered useless and forlorn and he had no idea where life would take him next. We now know that it would take him on to even greater victories as a trainer than he had known as a jockey but, as he lay in hospital in Camden on 28 November 1977, all that Mouse knew was pain and despair: the former came from his terrible injuries, while the latter came from a nagging feeling in his mind that his body was trying to tell him 'enough is enough'.

★

The Colonial Cup was a really big deal in racing back then and, as former jockey-turned-successful trainer and television pundit Ted Walsh recalls, it brought together the biggest stars of National Hunt racing from all over the globe to compete for a prize which, at the time, was the single biggest on offer anywhere:

> The Colonial Cup was a race first thought up in 1969 or 1970 and there was one hundred thousand dollars for winning it at a time when the Gold Cup was worth eight grand. Mrs duPont Scott, who was married to the great actor Randolph Scott and who was originally from the duPont pharmaceutical family, owned Camden in South Carolina, which was like owning Cheltenham – except it was bigger.
>
> She got this idea that she'd have this race and bring National Hunt horses from all over the world to run in it. There was this massive prize and all your expenses were paid to get out there. It was a great honour at that time to be asked to go and if you were associated with a top horse you went – no question. If they were to do something like that now, it would be the equivalent of running a two-million-dollar chase and paying for people to come and run in it.

Walsh says that the race was made even more attractive for British and Irish owners, trainers and jockeys, in that it was run more or less at the start of their season, so that if you had a decent horse for whom there were reasonable expectations of racing at the Cheltenham Festival the following March, they would have a chance to recover, in spite of their long journey to America for a tilt at this massive prize.

Tony Mullins, son of Paddy Mullins, and the jockey who rode Dawn Run in some of her biggest races, remembers that the legendary Irish racing and Gaelic games commentator, Mícheal O'Hehir, was the international liaison man for the event and that he, along with the Americans, decided which horses were invited from Ireland and the UK. Mullins says: 'We had one in it in 1970 and it was like going to the moon at the time for us. It was a horse called Herring Gull and when the white flag was raised, he ran out at the start and never even jumped a fence. We went all that way only for that to happen.'

Tom Busteed, who was then the amateur rider at Edward O'Grady's yard, also remembers those early days:

I travelled there once with Mícheal O'Hehir, 1974 I think it was. There were two horses sent from Ireland, one was from Toss Taaffe, called Yenesi, and he was ridden by Tommy Carberry. We sent out Golden Lancer for Mouse to ride and I went out for a couple of weeks to look after the horse. There were a load of Irish out there – Timmy Hyde and Edward [O'Grady] were there along with Mouse – a big contingent. We were well looked after and it was a really good trip.

Jonjo O'Neill says: 'It was worth a good few bob and it was a real adventure. The fences weren't as big as our ones, but they were bigger than hurdles and that's why you'd go out there with fast-ground horses. If they could jump a hurdle they'd handle it over there.'

Former American Champion Jockey, Doug Fout, still thinks with great fondness of those days when the race was in its prime:

It was so nice over the years that so many foreign horses and their connections came over from Britain and Ireland, because it added a real international flavour to the race. The other thing was that Camden was a big open course, which was fair for everyone and didn't really favour anyone. Also, the fences were more like those you guys [European jockeys] would be used to than those we were used to, so it was always interesting to see how it would shape up.

Fout, who is now a trainer in his own right in Middleburg, Virginia, looking after a mixed yard of jumpers and flat horses, recalls a time when the taking part was as important as the winning, with all the jockeys partying together: 'Your guys always seemed a bit rowdier than our guys, but there was a real fun flavour to the thing away from the serious racing.'

Having himself spent time with the legendary Fred Winter in England, Fout was only too well aware of the talent that would arrive in Camden every year in the shape of both horses and jockeys:

Fred trained horses for my grandmother and I went over there five or six times to see all the big races and ride out for him and everything, and I had worked with Dermot Weld on the Curragh in Ireland when I was sixteen as well, so I knew a lot about the racing over there and the guys who rode as well. When they came over here I was a contact point, and I got to bring them around to all the local bars and the parties that were on before and after the races. We had a lot of fun back then – a lot of drinkin' and dancin' and a lot of characters.

The whole thing was huge. You came down there five or six days before the racing and there was huge hype leading up to the race itself. The papers were full of it and at the time it was the biggest thing in the racing year. There was no Breeders' Cup then, so this was the cream of the crop in America. And, obviously, with the prize money it was huge, and a real big draw for foreign horses. There were some real good horses won there over the years – Crisp [famously nailed on the line at Aintree by Red Rum for the first of his three wins in the Grand National] won there and L'Escargot won there too.

★

In 1977, two English horses and one German lined up alongside nine runners from America to try and win that year's Cup. The 1977 *American Steeplechasing* annual tells us that Mouse Morris was aboard Down First (owned by Mrs Miles Valentine), while Jonjo O'Neill got the leg-up on Peter Easterby's Champion Hurdle winner, the great Sea Pigeon.

As it happened, the fateful 1977 race was won by local star, Café Prince, just returned from injury and ridden by Jerry Fishback, with Doug Fout's Bel Iman five and a half lengths back in second. Fout still has clear memories of the race and reveals that his horse was a doubt on race morning since he was running a temperature of 103 °F but, as both Bel Iman and Café Prince were fighting it out to be the Horse of the Year in America, the decision was taken to run him:

When the race got under way I remember tracking the leaders in about fourth place and I remember Mouse having his fall at the fourth fence. He sort of got blinded going into the fence and, if I remember correctly, it was a very bright sunny day and there were two fences as you came onto the home straight – those were two fences where the sun was right in your eyes. I'm sure Mouse's horse was blinded and fell because the sun made what was a four-foot fence into a ten-foot fence. Second time around my horse walked through one of them and nearly came down, but it was the first time around that caught Mouse. He was going easy enough at the time, but it was early in the race.

Mouse himself remembers the incident rather differently in that he was hit from behind on landing at the fourth fence and he reckons that his leg was actually broken before he hit the ground. The first thing he noticed after he hit the ground was the curious position of his right foot: 'I sat up and there was the sole of my left boot pointing up at me. I remember Adrian Maxwell [who had earlier that year trained Billycan to win the Irish Grand National with Mouse aboard] running up to me to see if I was all right and he turned very pale. I just told him to give me a fag and it'd be all right.' Misfortune also struck Jonjo at the fourteenth fence when Sea Pigeon, reportedly making his move to go and win the race at the time, also fell foul of the Camden obstacles. He recalls ruefully:

> Mouse and myself both got buried in the race. We were carted off to the hospital and both of us ended up on trolleys in the corridor because nobody would come and look at us because we had no insurance and there was nobody to vouch for us. We were both there with suspected broken legs. I was already after coming back having broken a leg and I thought the same thing had happened again because it had gone numb ... mine was OK, but Mouse had a very bad break and sadly, as it turned out, that was the start of the end for him. It wasn't very funny I can tell you, waiting in that corridor ... waiting for someone. It was really a very worrying few hours, but at least we had each other to talk to.

Mouse himself still curses that day in South Carolina. He was just beginning to make his mark among the ranks of paid jockeys. Having only just turned professional in the 1974–75 season, he was then the number one jockey at Edward O'Grady's increasingly prominent yard and already had two Champion Chase victories at Cheltenham under his belt, as well as a host of other big race wins. He says:

> Other than seeing my boot pointing up in the wrong direction, I don't remember much about the fall itself, except that both Jonjo and myself were shifted off to a big hospital in Camden by

ambulance. What I do remember after that is that the two of us were left there for a good while, because none of the medical people would touch us until the whole issue of payment or insurance was sorted. The two of us were in quite a deal of pain and I remember getting really worried. Eventually someone from the race committee came along and sorted everything out and we got treated.

I didn't know it at the time, but that race was going to have a big influence on my life after that. The big regret about that fall is that I was in the running with Tommy Carberry and Frank Berry to win the Irish jockeys' title, but that was the end of that.

Hardly surprising that Mouse pinpoints the 1977 Colonial Cup as the event that began to unravel his jockeying career. The Camden injury cost him a year out of racing and, even when he did come back, it was immediately apparent that things were never going to be the same. However, when it eventually came, his retirement would propel him into a new sphere in racing and he was to make his mark there as few others have done. For the road ahead lay in training and, although it was often a very rocky road, paved with doses of disappointment, tragedy, personal crises and pain, it was also a path to unimaginable success. For this new, as yet unimagined future, was to include the incalculable satisfaction of winning some of the biggest prizes racing has to offer.

2 The Lord

Mouse Morris comes from one of Ireland's oldest families, a fact of which he is rightly proud. His father, Michael Morris, the third Lord Killanin, ultimately became someone who could easily be described as Ireland's most prominent international diplomat, despite the fact that he never served the country in an official government capacity. He did serve Ireland greatly, however, in both his role as the sole Irish member of the International Olympic Council and, subsequently, as president of the same organisation.

History tells us that the Morris family settled in Galway in the fourteenth century and established itself as one of the fourteen fabled 'tribes of Galway'. Richard Morris was one of the family's most prominent early figures, becoming a bailiff in Galway in 1486, two years after the city's first charter from Richard III.

In his unpublished memoirs, Mouse's father says that early charac-terisations of some of the tribes had it that 'Joyces were merry, Blakes positive, Morrises were plausible.' The family fought with the Jacobites against the Williamites in 1691 and history records that the Morrises 'were definitely a mercantile family who had traded for generations with Spain.'

During Penal times, the Morrises had a smallholding near Spiddal, County Galway, and Lord Killanin's great grandfather, Martin Morris, was appointed the first Catholic High Sheriff of Galway in 1841. Martin's son and Lord Killanin's grandfather, Michel Morris, became Ireland's first Catholic High Chief Justice in 1885 and became the first Lord Morris and Killanin, 'one of the first hereditary peers of the twentieth century in 1900.'

Lord Killanin's father, Major the Hon. George Henry Morris, was an Irish nationalist and was educated at Edgbaston Oratory School, before being commissioned into the Rifle Brigade and fighting on the North-West frontier in India. He also served in the Boer War in 1899. Between 1908 and 1911 he was an instructor at the Irish Guards staff college and in 1913, at the age of forty-two, was promoted to Lieutenant Colonel. He married Dora Wesley Hall of Mount Morgan and Melbourne in Westminster Cathedral on 29 April 1913 and the aisles were lined by Irish Guardsmen in scarlet tunics for the occasion.

Dora Morris' family had emigrated to Australia in the 1830s from Herefordshire. Her father was James Wesley Hall, the first Managing Director of the Mount Morgan goldmine in Queensland and also Mayor of Mount Morgan. According to Lord Killanin's memoirs, his mother met a 'prematurely grey' George in 1912 while travelling in the west of Ireland.

Lord Killanin himself was born on 30 July 1914 and was allegedly the first Morris born outside Galway since the fifteenth century. The day prior to his birth had seen Austria declare war on Serbia in what was the start of the First World War. This conflict would have a huge bearing on the latest arrival to the Morris clan, since his father, George Morris, became one of the first high-profile casualties of battle when he was killed on 1 September 1914, near Villers Côterets in the retreat from Mons. He had travelled around the battlefield on horseback – 'superbly mounted on a grey horse', according to his regimental record. A stained-glass window in St Enda's Catholic Church in Spiddal commemorates his memory.

Mouse recalls that his father, Michael, was an only child and only three weeks old at the time his grandfather died: 'Going back, all our family were involved in law and my great, great grandfather, who was Michael as well, was the first Catholic Lord Chief Justice in Ireland. My own father was quite religious and he was proud of the fact that the Morris family had remained as Catholics when many other families had not.'

Martin Morris, Michael's uncle and the second Baron Killanin, had remained a bachelor until his death on 19 August 1927, aged sixty-one. An MP for Galway, he was the last Lieutenant of the county and a County Council member until 1922. He had moved to London during the Irish War of Independence in 1922 when his Protestant chauffeur,

Ruttledge, claimed he had been threatened by the IRA. The family's Spiddal mansion was subsequently burnt down on 23 April 1923. When Martin died, Michael Morris inherited the title Lord Killanin. Although he inherited the title in 1927, it was not until 1935, aged twenty-one, that he was summoned to the House of Lords. There he initially sat on Tory benches, but transferred to cross benches and was thereafter never a member of a political party.

According to Lord Killanin, after his father's death his mother 'led a fairly nomadic life between Spiddal and visiting the wives and widows of those who were at the front.' She spent considerable time at Knepp Castle near Horsham, the home of Peter, son of Sir Merrick and Lady Burrell. Peter was later manager of the National Stud in Ireland and England.

He also recalls that the house in Spiddal 'had been a small, Georgian-type house – a summer country house – for the Morrises who lived in the city of Galway in Lower Dominick Street, as was the custom of most of "the Tribes".' His uncle had enlarged the house into 'a gigantic Hiberno-Romanesque three-floor building with a copper dome.'

In due course, Lord Killanin's mother was remarried to Gerard Tharp. They had a daughter, Philippa, in 1918 and a son, John, in 1923. John later became an RAF pilot and went missing while flying at night in a Beaufighter operating out of Tunis during the Second World War. He was presumed killed in 1943. Gerard Tharp was the nephew of Monty Tharp and Bea-Annabella Lucy Gent-Tharp who owned the Limekiln gallops in Newmarket, 'virtually the first natural all-weather gallops', sold in due course to the Jockey Club.

Killanin recalls that Gerard Tharp 'was not interested in racing'. However he himself was keen on horses and, in 1923 while living at Wick Street House between Painswick and Stroud in Gloucestershire, he rode a Welsh pony called Thunderer. He also recounts that the family moved back and forth between London and the country and points out that, 'although we were not very wealthy, the large London houses were usually staffed with between eight and ten servants.'

He maintains that his stepfather, along with most of the country, looked askance at those professionally involved in racing – 'social association with trainers was taboo' – but that he met many jockeys and stable lads when he went to mass, 'for, needless to say, many were Irish compatriots.' He also used to hunt with the Newmarket and Thurlow hounds and reveals that, while he loved the riding, he 'was never so keen on the kill.'

In the light of the fact that his son went on to become a noted jockey and trainer, one of Lord Killanin's stories has an amusing slant:

> One day after hunting I invited Bill Rickaby, the former jockey, back to Chippenham [the then family home] for a cup of tea. He did not receive a very warm reception and I was instructed clearly never to invite a jockey home! How my stepfather would be shocked to know that one of our sons, after a successful career as a qualified rider [amateur] in Ireland and a season with the great trainer of horses and jockeys, 'Frenchie' Nicholson, was to become a professional steeplechase jockey who had five Grand National rides, besides winning the Irish National and Gold Cup at Fairyhouse in 1977. That victory actually gave me a heart attack, so I wonder what would it have done to Gerard Tharp?

Unfortunately Gerard Tharp did suffer sudden death from a heart attack in 1932, but before that Lord Killanin had been sent to Summerfield School in 1923 and on to Eton in 1928. He was, he maintains, 'very interested in boxing' at Eton and represented the school, playing junior rugby there as well.

At Eton he would slip across the river to watch the Windsor Races and assisted Clive Graham, later the *Daily Express* racing correspondent, in keeping a book: 'I had learnt not to bet, but realised that most bookmakers seemed to be rich and, between us all, we kept an illegal book which earned a few pounds extra each half term.' He also met Charlie Chaplin and Gandhi, both of whom visited the school in his time. He was, he says, 'not rich compared with some Etonians', although he did enjoy a 'very large personal allowance of £500 per annum.'

After Eton he was invited to go up to Magdalene College, Cambridge, by the Master, A. B. Ramsay, due to his apparent interest in rowing. As Ramsay said at the time, 'We are anxious to have rowing men at Magdalene.' Upon arrival, he took a taxi to the college boat-house, as he did not know where it was. While paying the taxi-driver he was seen by a third-year who told him, in no uncertain terms, that if he was going to row for Magdalene he should not come down by taxi, but should run the short distance to the boat-house. Killanin replied that 'if he did not want to see me, I would be very happy to leave and I turned around and ran back to Magdalene. That was the last I ever saw of the River Cam as far as being an oarsman was concerned.'

At university he initially read history but switched to a general degree in English and history. He was involved in the famous Footlights Club, which staged many plays and comedies during his time, becoming Club President in his second year and helping with 'set design, acting and compèring'. As literary editor on *Varsity*, he learnt 'the first rudiments of popular journalism' and contributed at the same time to the short-lived glossy, *Oxford and Cambridge.*

His first stirrings of interest in the Olympic movement came about at this time too, due to encountering Lord Burghley, Olympic hurdler and former Magdalene student, who 'was responsible for me being elected a member of the International Olympic Committee.'

Killanin was very much a pacifist while at Cambridge, which he says was due to 'the destruction of World War I' and 'the blackness of the clothes of my youth' in the aftermath of his father's death. The accent which remained with him throughout his adult life was 'the accent of Oxbridge in the thirties'.

His Oxbridge education was to introduce him to characters who would become infamous in the course of time – particularly in the world of espionage. Two of the most notable of these were double agents Guy Burgess and Donald McLean, both of whom spied on Britain for Russia while apparently working for MI6. He remembers: 'Guy Burgess I had known from Eton days – I always thought Guy was grubby and ill-kempt. I saw him frequently during the war in clubs and pubs in London and I knew he had left-wing views.' Three weeks prior to Burgess fleeing to the USSR, Killanin actually bumped into him – 'he was very drunk' – near the Stephen's Green Club in Dublin and Burgess told him he had had a nervous breakdown. He also spoke to Burgess on the telephone while on a business trip to Moscow in 1962.

Of Donald McLean, he says 'nothing could be more respectable or traditional in his bearing. I do not remember McLean being friendly with Burgess as, at that time, they appeared so different', but he says he 'got to know Anthony Blunt quite well as we frequently met at parties.' Blunt, of course, was 'outed' as a Russian spy many years later.

On leaving college, Killanin's initial inclination was to move into journalism. The *Varsity* gossip column of October 1935 noted that it had 'at last discovered why it is that Cambridge is feeling so empty at the moment. It is because Lord Killanin has gone down.' It was time to get a real job.

In 1935 he was introduced to Lord Beaverbook (of Express Newspapers) by Valentine Castlerosse, whose sister, Lady Cicely Vesey, was Killanin's godmother. He rather unkindly describes Beaverbrook as 'little gnome of a man' but, even so, he was given a six-month trial by J. B. Wilson, News Editor of the *Daily Express*, at £5 per week – somewhat below the union minimum of £9 per week.

He remembers that there were two lists in the newsroom: one of forbidden words, and the other of people who must not be mentioned. However he enjoyed the work and 'covered every sort of story – murders, suicides, robberies and scandal' and, 'over pints of mild and bitter, I had an immense education' from senior journalists in the Poppin's Court, a pub near the office in Fleet Street.

Killanin was fired from the *Express* some months later because he failed to get a story checked by the Irish High Commissioner, John Dulanty. He always maintained he had confirmed the story, but he got the heave-ho nonetheless and almost immediately joined the rival paper, the *Daily Mail*, where he earned some £9 per week. He also worked on their Sunday paper, the *Sunday Dispatch*, for which he covered the abdication of King Edward VIII.

In one amusing incident of that period, he remembers taking John Wayne out drinking in London. The two had to leave the legendary Fleet Street pub, El Vino's, since the staff wouldn't serve men wearing hats. Killanin recalls that 'Wayne had a hair or toupee problem' and wouldn't remove his hat, so they both got thrown out.

In August 1937 he left for Shanghai to cover the Japanese invasion for the *Daily Mail*. He docked in Hong Kong and made his way up to Canton before later getting a ship to Shanghai. From his hotel, the Metropole, he could see a lot of the Japanese–Chinese fighting and he recalls that 'Chinese press conferences were in the morning and more formal, while the Japanese held theirs in the afternoon – accompanied by a good deal of whiskey.'

While in China he also went to Nanking where General Chiang Kai-shek was based. Many foreign missions were advising the Chinese there, but he managed to meet the General, who he describes as 'austere'. He later returned to Shanghai but when the city was captured by the Japanese, he went to Japan 'to pick up some political and other stories' and he says he did not realise at the time that he had made his name in Fleet Street as a result of the by-lines which appeared almost daily in the paper.

In Tokyo he interviewed Minister of War, General Suetsugu – 'very conservative' – and the Minister for the Navy and later Prime Minister, Admiral Yonai. To have had access to such men in the period immediately before the Second World War was big news back then and Killanin's reputation as a serious journalist was by now well established.

On his way back to the UK, he travelled via the USA and he was actually met in Hollywood by John Ford 'whose father had emigrated from near Spiddal' and who would later direct the film, *The Quiet Man*, starring none other than John Wayne.

When he returned to Fleet Street he was given a pay increase and made assistant to J. Wilson [Jack] Broadbent, the political and diplomatic correspondent of the *Daily Mail*. Later he was to take over the political news and gossip column of the *Sunday Dispatch* and was among the journalists sent to Downing Street on 26 September 1938 to hear Chamberlain's infamous 'peace in our time' speech, after the so-called Munich agreement with Hitler. It was also around this period that he made a speech in the House of Lords supporting the return to Britain of the Irish Treaty ports – a speech for which he was 'criticised by the assembly'.

In 1938 Killanin edited *Four Days*, a book on the Munich agreement, and soon after joined the Territorial Army, amidst concern over increasing Nazi power. He was commissioned as a second lieutenant in the Queen's Westminsters and Civil Service Rifles (TA) and, when war broke out in 1939, and he was mobilised, his company initially guarding London targets under threat from an IRA campaign.

He had actually been on holiday in Spiddal at the time of mobilisation. There he spent time with George Thompson, a lecturer in Classics and locum at University College, Galway, as well as novelist, Francis Stuart, who (it later emerged) had Nazi sympathies.

Around 1940, Killanin was Company Commander at St Catherine's Docks, later wiring the coast between Newport and Swansea against German invasion. Subsequently, he served in the 49th (West Riding) Infantry Division in Yorkshire, making friends among the monks at Ampleforth where he would later send his sons to be educated. He was Adjutant to the battalion, then given command of HQ Company, a non-combatant rifle company in a rifle battalion, before becoming Brigade

Major to the 30th Armoured Brigade. In due course he was transferred to Warminster where he acted essentially as a staff officer. 'I was more suited to be a staff officer than a commanding officer,' he noted later.

Lord Killanin was heavily involved in the preparations for the Normandy assault in 1942, but found it 'fascinating' that he was allowed on leave a fortnight before D-Day to travel to Dublin. 'Security for the D-Day and Normandy landings to this day astounds me,' he commented later. However, by the time he was shipped out to France 'it was', he says, 'comparatively quiet and safe on the beaches.'

His was more of an organisational than a combat role in Normandy and he had to collect together tanks from various regiments, count casualties and prepare for the next move as the Allied forces tried to break down German resistance. On one occasion he was accosted by one of the main allied commanders, General Montgomery, who was out on a motorbike trying to find General Dempsey's Second Army HQ. 'Monty and his entourage stopped for directions and I later discovered I had sent him directly to the German lines.' He 'hardly dared show his face for a few days', but Montgomery was 'safe and sound', despite the mistake.

Although essentially in a non-combat role, he was still involved in the battle for Le Harve, where the 30th Brigade mopped up pockets of German soldiers left behind by their retreating comrades, and he later fought at the Battle of the Falaise Gap, which he describes as the 'beginning of the end of the German Army'. At the war's end, he was to be among the first British officers to discover the horrors of Belsen concentration camp.

★

Killanin's memoirs reveal that, in spite of an MBE for his wartime endeavours, he 'pulled some strings to get out of the Army as quickly as I could' after the war ended and engineered a speedy return to Ireland where, at the Galway Races in August 1945, he was to meet his future wife. He recalls:

> I was taken to the Galway Races … and I did not then realise it was there that my father had met my mother, nor indeed that it was where I was to meet my wife Sheila Dunlop [the daughter of the

Church of Ireland rector of Oughterard] while lunching with the same Pierce Joyce who had proposed to my mother in 1912 [and had taken her to Galway where his father met her].

Sheila had actually served in the armed forces during the war as well, working at the highly secretive Bletchley Park complex where British code-breakers cracked the Germans' Enigma coding machines and probably brought the conflict to an end faster than would otherwise have been the case. She was later awarded an MBE for her work there although she never spoke about it publicly, since, for many years, she was still governed by the Official Secrets Act. The fact that both had MBEs made them more than a little unique in Irish society.

The future Lady Killanin's grandfather, H. W. D. Dunlop, was the founder of Lansdowne Road Rugby Football Club and laid out the international grounds at the site. After their marriage in 1945 Killanin remained true to his love of Galway and the couple would divide their time between their Galway and Dublin homes – the latter coincidentally found in Lansdowne Road. As a sign of his first loyalty, however, the Killanin cars always carried Galway registration plates.

Just a year after their marriage, while lunching in the Garrick Club in London, Killanin was asked by George Wilson if he would join the board of Irish Shell. He agreed and stayed on as a director there until 1984, receiving some £100 per annum for his services.

For Killanin it was to be the start of an energetic business career: in 1958 he became a member of Lloyds, as well as a director of Chubb Ireland and Chairman of Bovril Ireland, amongst other companies. He estimated that he was a director of between thirty and forty companies in the end, including the Ulster Bank, and Beamish and Crawford in Cork. Even so, it did not make him a rich man, as he records ruefully: 'I seem to be very good at making money for other people and not for myself.'

Throughout the 1950s he was to become quite involved in the film business and worked on *The Quiet Man* with John Ford, as well as the Jack Hawkins police movie, *Gideon's Day*, amongst others. His eldest son, Redmond, is himself now a movie producer with a string of illustrious credits to his name, including many of Neil Jordan's films, such as *Interview with a Vampire*, *Michael Collins*, *The Butcher Boy* and *In Dreams*, as well as Ken Loach's Cannes Palme d'Or winner, *The Wind that Shakes the Barley*. Redmond says that his father's interest in film-making was more of a pastime than anything else: 'He formed a company called Four Provinces Productions with John Ford, Tyrone Power and the architect, Michael Scott, and they did quite a few films, including a version of *The Playboy of the Western World* with Siobhán McKenna. But it was like a hobby with him, it certainly was not his livelihood.'

It was in the early 1950s that his involvement with the Olympic movement really took off – a role that would ultimately define Lord Killanin. Having been President of the Olympic Council of Ireland, he was elected to the International Olympic Committee (IOC) in 1952. American businessman, Avery Brundage, was President in those years and he ruled with an iron fist. When Killanin and some of his colleagues made secret contact with the Chinese, then not competing in the Olympics, Brundage deliberately appointed a new IOC member in Taiwan in a move deliberately designed to infuriate Beijing.

In 1966 he became IOC Head of Protocol and, in the following year, head of the Press Commission. His close friend and co-author of two books based on the Olympics, John Rodda, recalls a man who ran into his fair share of controversy when he eventually succeeded Brundage as the President of the IOC at the start of the 1972 Games in Munich:

> During his years as President of the International Olympic Committee, from 1972 to 1980, he shaped a truly worldwide movement. He was elected a few days before terrorists murdered members of the Israeli team at the Munich Olympic Village. Other crises he faced included the occasion when the host city, Denver, opted out in the midst of preparations for the 1976 Winter Games, and a saga of corruption surrounding the same year's Summer Games in Montreal. Having framed a new commercial deal on the Olympic event, he concentrated on preparing for the 1980 Moscow Games. Then, on Boxing Day 1979 at home in Dublin, he heard the news of the Soviet invasion of Afghanistan. From then on he struggled to save the Games as 62 of the 142 member countries decided to boycott the Soviet capital.

His children remember the hullabaloo with clarity and Redmond says that his father was under extreme pressure during this period, as the

Americans used their worldwide influence to try and derail Moscow's sporting showpiece:

> During the crisis before the Moscow Games he was going from Carter to Brezhnev and Brezhnev to Carter, it was high politics. He was under big pressure – he had the heart attack at the same time, but I don't know was that more to do with Mouse winning the Irish Grand National, or him being at the centre of one of the biggest international controversies of the era.

His daughter-in-law, former RTÉ presenter Thelma Mansfield, remembers that at the time she was even taking flak from colleagues at work because of what was going on: 'Even where I worked, people were really obnoxious about it and I'd get stick, so you can only imagine the sort of abuse the family were getting,' she says. Her husband, John, was at those Games and still remembers vividly the no-win situation his father was in: 'I went to Moscow with him for what were his last Olympics as IOC President. It was very sad. I remember a Russian coming up to us and saying, "Why do you hate us so much?"'

The Moscow Games went ahead eventually, despite the 62-country boycott, and Killanin retired from the IOC Presidency not long after, but Rodda reckons that the high politics which surrounded those Olympics were not his lowest moment in the job:

> The 1976 Montreal Games were a nightmare for him. Costs overran hugely and for nine months Killanin spoke every Friday to the Quebec minister, Victor Goldbloom, who detailed the week's progress. But, with several IOC members, he began secret planning for an emergency alternative competition in the Ruhr, just in case.
>
> Then, just six days before the Games began, Canada vetoed the Taiwan team's participation. Killanin knew that if nationalist China was thrown out the United States would probably call a boycott. And, as if all that was not bad enough, the IOC failed to address the protests over New Zealand's rugby tour of South Africa and some twenty-two African countries pulled out of Montreal. That was one of his saddest moments. He did, however, fight diligently to keep South Africa out of the Olympic movement until apartheid was gone.

Lord Killanin presided over a very volatile period in the history of the Olympic movement, contending not only with highly charged political matters, but also problems within the sport, since the issue of amateurism was coming under close scrutiny. Even so, John Rodda's summation of his IOC career is short and sweet: 'Killanin was the man who opened the door on the world's biggest sporting event, shed a little light and fended off crises in Montreal and Moscow.'

Browsing the man's memoirs, his life sometimes seems like a *Who's Who* of the world, straddling, as it does, sport, politics, literature, the film industry and business. The legions of famous people he met over the years is amazing – as are some of his observations of them. He says, 'The most vital, pragmatic politician that I have met in Eastern Europe is President Ceausescu of Romania, which I visited in 1974. He is very small, but highly intellectual. I would think very ruthless when need be.' Killanin also met the Shah of Iran twice and found him to be an 'extremely arrogant' man.

When he was the Honorary Consul General for Monaco in Ireland he was asked by Prince Rainier to provide advice on procedure in accepting an unofficial invitation to a concert given by Our Lady's Choral Society in Croke Park, and this led to the semi-official visit of the Prince and Princess Grace to Ireland in 1961. He had previously met Princess Grace – then actress Grace Kelly - at MGM studios at Elstree in England and was immediately 'struck by her beauty'. He later helped her arrange a visit to her ancestors' homestead near Newport, County Mayo and visited the royal couple in Monaco on a number of occasions.

On a later visit to Ireland, Rainier and Grace stayed at Carton House and Killanin played many rounds of golf at Portmarnock or the Hermitage with the Prince, who he recalled as 'pretty intelligent, although conservative, and extremely good company.' When Princess Grace died tragically on 14 September 1982, he attended her funeral in Monaco along with President Hillery. 'We had lost a good friend, but a very sad one,' he commented at the time.

A very busy man in the racing world, he served on Galway Racecourse Committee from 1947 (taking the chair between 1969 and 1985), as well as being a member of the Irish National Hunt Steeple-chase Committee and stewarding at various meetings. From 1970 to 1972 he was an elected member of the Turf Club, stewarding for it between 1980 and 1982. This, in turn, led to him being nominated by Charles Haughey to chair the government commission on the Irish Thoroughbred horse-breeding industry. 'I was one of the kings of the reorganisation of flat racing,' he later declared.

Reflecting on their father's status as one of Ireland's most famous unpaid ambassadors, Redmond says that he does not now think the Killanin children really understood what he actually was:

> I don't think we appreciated the fact that our father was a lord. He was just a dad to us. He was away quite a bit, but he was good fun. I'm not sure any of us were that close to him, but he was a very active man and we spent a lot of time fishing on the river in Spiddal and in the lakes around there. We did a bit of shooting, too, and he was very keen on those old-style picnics – the wicker baskets and all that.
>
> I suppose it is only really now that I appreciate how extraordinary our childhood was and how extraordinary he was. I have to say that his unpublished memoir is funny in a way, because it is like a list of who he knew, but it is not written in any sort of an affected way. He just tells it like it was for him. His life was extraordinary. It was privileged in a way, but even so I think we are all fairly down-to-earth people.

Redmond inherited the title when his father died on 25 April 1999, after fighting bravely against the effects of Parkinson's disease for several years. However he does not use the appellation 'Lord Killanin', as he explains:

> I don't use the title much, for various reasons. It doesn't really mean that much any more and, for example, it does not entitle you to sit in the House of Lords any more, thanks to Tony Blair. I also find it very difficult to change my name as a professional. I've been using my own name as a screen credit for forty or more years and I'd be a bit embarrassed to change it. I think my Dad was a bit embarrassed by it too, although he inherited the title at the age of thirteen and he lived the whole of his life with it. All his professional life he was Lord Killanin, so it was easier that way for him. I would hate the title to disappear, but I don't use it much.

Living in Ireland now, it seems slightly archaic. Oddly enough, I find I'm more comfortable with it in Galway than anywhere else.

The name Lord Killanin may not see much use in the present but, even now, it is still one of the best-known names in Irish society. Although he was a lord, he was considerably more popular amongst his fellow Irishmen and women than many a politician.

For the family, there was a terribly proud moment in September 2007 when Galway Racecourse opened the Killanin Stand – a new €22-million facility – named after the person who racecourse chairman, Ray Rooney, described as 'an outstanding contributor to sport and to racing – and in particular to Galway Races.' Killanin's children and grandchildren were there for the occasion, but unfortunately his wife, Sheila, had passed away the previous March. Without a doubt she would have been hugely satisfied to see her late husband being recognised in this way by his own people.

3   Childhood

Unlike many people who have had a similarly privileged background, Mouse is not afraid to admit that his early childhood was idyllic, with a good deal of it spent in the family's ancestral home in County Galway, just outside the village of Spiddal in the Connemara Gaeltacht. And, while it might not appear that this period of his life had a huge bearing on his subsequent career, in many ways he is still in tune with the wild west coast of Ireland, as if attached by an invisible umbilical cord.

He may not be a *gaeilgeoir* in the true sense of the word, but his acute awareness of his Irish heritage – much like his father's – and his cultural leanings, including a love of traditional music and an appreciation for the unique landscape of the western seaboard (as evidenced by his little-known prowess as a photographer), mark Mouse out a as Connacht man.

His childhood in Galway is still a vivid, living thing for him and going there now – as he often does – brings back fantastic memories of a time when life, even as the son of a lord, was a simple, precious and innocent thing. 'I remember Spiddal well', he says, 'and even now when I go back there I get flashbacks to how it was when we were children. We lived in the "Big House" outside Spiddal and we had a river, acres of land and the sea. It was a paradise playground for children.'

★

Mouse and his twin brother, John, were born four years after the Killanin's eldest child, Redmond, and just two years after sister, Deborah, arrived on the scene. The twins were born twenty minutes apart, with Mouse being the elder. John's memories of the time are fresh:

We undoubtedly had a privileged childhood but, by the same token, we used to go around in our bare feet like the local kids. We used to play on the river and I suppose that these days we were playing what would be considered very dangerous games. We used to make little boats out of fish boxes and launch them on the Spiddal River. We were very Huckleberry Finn-type characters and I definitely don't think we were treated any differently from any other kids growing up in the village around the same time.

Redmond, similarly, has very fond memories of a childhood bathed in the inherent innocence typical of Ireland at that time, but greatly enhanced by the sheer freedom and excitement their environment provided:

I actually went to school in Spiddal initially – to the local National School and then the boys' school for a few years before I was sent to school in Dublin. To us, as children, 'the Big House' seemed much bigger then, but has got considerably smaller as we got older. I certainly had a very happy childhood in Spiddal and even when we came to school in Dublin, we always went back there on holidays. We might know different now, but in those days we did not in any way consider ourselves as having a privileged childhood. That was just the way it was and all the people I grew up with there are still my friends. There might have been a bit of the 'Mac an Lord' thing going on in the village, but we were not differentiated from the other children. I remember doing all the normal things, like going to the post office to collect the mail, and going into Hughes' pub to get the can of milk and things like that. It was a great place to grow up.

John says that it was in early childhood in Spiddal that Mouse had his first real exposure to horses, since there were always ponies around and recalls: 'The man who used to look after the ponies back then was John Feeney, who was from Spiddal and was related to the John Ford who, of course, was a good friend of the Killanins.' Mouse himself says:

My father co-produced several movies with John Ford. Ford actually claimed he was a relative of ours, but I'm not sure about that. They did films such as like *The Quiet Man*, *The Rising of the Moon*, and so forth. The two were great friends and Ford's mother was what they called the 'wet nurse' back in those days and she lived near us in Spiddal.

And, as Redmond remembers it:

John Ford was a friend of my father's and the first film set I was ever on was *The Quiet Man*. We just took that sort of thing in our stride. I mean we had John Wayne coming to the house and Tyrone Power would have been there too. I do remember being a little in awe of these people – not so much for who they were but for what they were involved with. To me, as a child, John Ford was just a man with an eye-patch, who pretended to come from Spiddal. He was John's godfather, but he was just an ordinary guy.

One of my Dad's horses actually took part in *The Quiet Man* – it was the horse which John Wayne rode on in the famous race scene, shot near Renvyle. It was actually the last horse my Dad owned because he pretty much gave up riding when the children came along.

If Lord Killanin had given up on his riding and hunting career, he was still very much involved in other horsey things, being the Chairman of the Galway Racecourse, as well as playing a leading role at the time in the Connemara Pony Association. 'Mouse and the rest of us were always brought to the Connemara Pony Show in Clifden every year,' John says.

As the children grew up, their full-time life in Spiddal came to an end, since their parents moved them to their Dublin home in Lansdowne Road where their education would begin in earnest. Unfortunately for Mouse, what followed was to turn into a terrible nightmare.

Initially things were fine and the twins, Mouse and John, followed Redmond into Miss Meredith's School in Baggot Street and, following that, to St Conleth's School on Clyde Road. From there they would be sent on to one of the most prominent and expensive Catholic public schools in England – Ampleforth in Yorkshire. Redmond tells a story that exemplifies the sort of clientele who went there: 'One of the boys went to confession and told the priest, "Bless me father for I have sinned.

I went to bed with a lady", to which the priest replied, "Lady who?"'
Redmond goes on:

> If the normal train of events had unfolded, we probably would
> have been sent to Eton like Dad had been. But he had not
> enjoyed being a Catholic at Eton and, having met the monks up
> at Ampleforth during his war years, he made good friends there;
> I'd say that was why we were sent. I had a good time there, but
> Mouse definitely didn't.

While his two siblings were still in Dublin, they were regularly
dispatched after school for riding lessons with the legendary Irish show-
jumping heroine and noted horsewoman, Iris Kellet. John recalls that
himself and Mouse used to walk to Kellet's, which was on Mespil Road
at the time: 'I remember he was always playing at being a jockey there,
but I don't know where that came from. Certainly my father had been
a good huntsman in his youth with the Galway Blazers, so there was
some tradition there. But in terms of wanting to become a jockey, I don't
think even Mouse knows where it came from.'

Redmond claims he does not really have much recollection of
Mouse as a child in Dublin, probably because he was already in
Ampleforth, but he does remember him going to Iris Kellet's and
'being harangued about having his stirrups too high.' Even at that
stage, his eldest brother reckons, he had the urge to be a jockey,
although he didn't know it himself: 'It was all very prim and proper
down there and he got a lot of stick because he was always edging the
stirrups up a notch.'

Mouse was to get his nickname at Kellet's, where family friend and
future amateur jockey Timmy Jones – a noted joker who would later
gain infamy as the man who rode Gay Future to victory – started calling
young Michael Morris, 'Mickey Morris', his in turn becoming 'Mickey
Mouse', and then, simply, 'Mouse'.

In any event, the whole Morris family was involved with ponies at
some point in their childhood, as Redmond recalls: 'All of us went
through the horsey thing – I had been sent to Ian Dudgeon out in
Sandyford – and we all took it quite seriously for a while, but I can't
remember any one moment where he announced he was going to be a
jockey or anything like that.'

Whatever ambitions Mouse may have had at this stage, Ampleforth beckoned and while Redmond had done well there and enjoyed the experience, his little brother's time there was to be very fraught, if ultimately career-shaping. Mouse remembers:

> I was twelve or thirteen when I was sent to Ampleforth. John and myself were sent at the same time, but I hated it. I was actually dyslexic but nobody even knew what that was at the time. They just thought I was stupid. It was my mum who actually discovered it much later. She read an article in *The Observer* or somewhere about this new discovery and they sent me off to get tested and it turned out that was the problem. There were no remedial schools or anything like that back in those days. The St John of God School in Orwell Road started something all right later on, but the horse had bolted as far as I was concerned by then. Nowadays there are all sorts of things you can get to help. One of my own sons has it too, but he was able to get different lenses for his glasses and something as simple as that allowed him to cope. A simple solution.
>
> I hated every minute of Ampleforth – apart from the sport. I couldn't read English, not to mind Latin or French or anything. In those days they got you to stand up and read and if you got anything wrong you got a whack across the head. I got a lot of whacks. When you're getting bashed about the place like that, it is no surprise that you've no interest in it. I was bottom of the class and going nowhere. Eventually I decided I wasn't going back. I told my parents I didn't want to go and they were trying to tell me it would be all right when I settled back in, but that was never going to persuade me. We had a tree house in the back garden in Lansdowne Road and I hid there until it was too late to go back, too late to catch the plane. I had had a breakdown before that – I didn't know it, but I was in bits – and my parents knew something was wrong, seriously wrong.

John has – understandably – vivid memories of the time and of the agonies his twin was going through and recalls being 'very protective' of Mouse during their spell at Ampleforth, mainly because his brother was being bullied:

He was a good-looking boy and he was being bullied both by those who fancied him and also by people who teased him because he couldn't read properly. We used to have to read our essays out in front of the class and I remember one day devising a scheme to put a stop to that. I wrote an essay and I incorporated the old cock-and-pullet joke – the one where there's a man on a bus with his cock and pullet but they escape and he roars out 'catch my cock and pullet'. The other boys loved it, but the monks were horrified and I don't think we were asked to read out our essays after that.

John's plan had been to stop something which he thought was manifestly unfair and unnecessary and it worked because, as he says: 'it prevented Mouse the embarrassment of having to go through the agony which it must have been for him.' Hiding up the tree in Lansdowne Road was, in essence, his cry for help. When, in John's words, he 'refused to come down', their parents realised something had to be done. Mouse says:

> In fairness to them, they didn't send me back. Instead they found me a job with a guy called Brian Cooper who used to train horses in Portmarnock. I used to go out there early in the morning and I got school grinds at home in the afternoon. I never actually did any exams and in fact I think I probably cracked up when I did the mock O-Level exams at Ampleforth but there was no more of it after that. I was good at sport – rugby, boxing and shooting – I am naturally a competitive person – but school wasn't for me.

It is probably indicative of the Killanins' forward thinking that Mouse was not the only member of the family to be excused completing his education. Redmond tells of having failed his second-year exams at Trinity, but being thrown a lifeline by his father:

> I wasn't particularly academic and I kind of knew I wanted to get into the film business. A friend of Dad's was working on a film in Ireland and I remember Dad saying, 'Look, I think what you should do is give up university and go and work on the movie and try and make a career for yourself.'

My parents were very sensible about Mouse too, Mother in particular. She was a rock – a formidable rock – but I always admired the two of them for being so realistic when it came to both my career and to Mouse's.

It might have been terribly frustrating for Lord and Lady Killanin to see two of their sons fail to finish their educations, but at least they had the foresight to realise that both Redmond and Mouse were wasting their time at university and school, respectively, and that at least it would be better to see them doing something they desperately wanted to do. That both men have turned out to be remarkably successful in their careers is a testament to the soundness of their judgement and their willingness to do their best for their children, even if that meant turning their backs on the perceived wisdom of their day, which dictated that children should do as they were told, without exception.

4   Jockey: A Different Life

Getting the 32A bus to Portmarnock from Lower Abbey Street at 6.30am every morning is not something most sixteen-year-olds would find an attractive proposition. However, still counting his blessings that he did not have to go back to his torturous existence at Ampleforth, but was now on a path to his chosen life as a jockey, Mouse had no problems with such relative discomfort. He endured those journeys without demur, eventually progressing to a Honda 50, and began to get into the rhythm of a racing stable – a rhythm that would stay with him throughout his professional life. He says:

> I worked with Brian Cooper for a couple of years before my father fixed it up through a friend of his, John Hislop – who was a sports writer and amateur jockey – for me to go to Frenchie Nicholson's yard in Cheltenham. I was sixteen by then and I wanted to be a jockey. In fact I always wanted to be a jockey and even at school a few of us used to keep a scrapbook full of oul' racing stuff – pictures and that.
>
> Myself and a fellow called Colin Dixon used to get into terrible trouble over it. But there was no problem going back to England this time – because it was something I wanted to do. My parents were one hundred and ten per cent behind me and, while it probably killed them that I was such an academic failure, they were really supportive. For some parents, especially those with the sort of background mine had, having a son become a jockey was not the 'done thing', but they backed me all the way. I was lucky that they were not blinkered and from the time they realised I was leaving school they did nothing but encourage me.

Having experienced life at Cooper's racing stable, the regime at Frenchie Nicholson's was not greatly different, but this time he just had to fall out of bed and he was at work. As Mouse says:

> The work at Nicholson's was very hard, but I didn't mind it at all. I was like a pig in shit, to be honest. Frenchie was very good with jockeys and, in my time, Tony Murray was there, Pat Eddery was there, and Frenchie was noted for not only being a good trainer of horses, but of jockeys too. That was something John Hislop would have advised the old man about. You got no pay back then, just your keep, so the folks had to send over a few bob, but I suppose it was a lot less expensive for them than Ampleforth had been.

Mouse did not do much race-riding over there at all and only really rode out. In a curious turn of events, his first race-ride was over the same Cheltenham fences that would mean so much to him in his riding and training careers. The fact that Nicholson's yard was situated just outside Prestbury village – out at the back of the racetrack near the water jump – was also one of the reasons why Mouse would become infatuated with the place. In his words:

> It is all housing estates there now, but back then it was a fine set-up, with thirty or forty boxes. I still go back to the local pub every year – The Plough – during the Festival meeting. I was actually there when the first big foot-and-mouth epidemic broke out in 1967 and Frenchie sent myself and a few others down to Pau in France for a couple of months, which was a good experience, and I rode quite a bit down there.

However his time in England was to be short. Even though he remembers this period of his life with extreme fondness, he was still a stranger in a strange land and wanted to come home. He recalls:

> After two years with Frenchie, he got me a job back in Ireland with Willie O'Grady [in Tipperary]. There was a vacancy for an amateur there and Willie took me on. Willie was a star, even if he liked a drink or two. He was very good to me and was very much a father figure. By then, somehow, I don't believe I actually ever felt

I was going to make it as a jockey, but Willie seemed to think I had something and I ended up staying there for years. As I say, Willie was like a second daddy to me and I used to drive him around the place and be his gofer.

Demi O'Byrne was then a vet but is now the main auction bidder in major sales rings for the Coolmore breeding empire in Fethard, County Tipperary, run by John Magnier. He says he first met Mouse around 1969 when the young man had just arrived at Willie O'Grady's:

Willie had the great Kinloch Brae at the time and I remember the horse was due to run at Punchestown one day and I got word late in the evening from Tim Finn that all was not well with him. Mouse had driven Willie home from wherever they had been and it was that night that I first got talking to Mouse. It was a very important mission for me that night because I was the local vet and had to try and sort things out. In any event the horse never ran the following day. But that was the first time I met him and we became great friends.

He was an amateur jockey back then, but our real friendship developed through the hunting. He was a devil to go to hounds – loved it. We hunted an awful lot and he could ride as good as anyone – as good as Timmy Hyde or any of them. That year was a watershed. I went to America to work as a vet in 1971 and Willie died in 1972, just after I arrived home. Mouse turned professional then in 1974.

It was not insignificant that it was Mouse who was driving Willie O'Grady that night. He was a really nice young fella and Willie was mad about him. Driving Willie around and listening to him, he would have picked up an awful lot, because Willie was one of the greatest horsemen of all time. I hero-worshipped Willie too. That would be some sort an explanation as to why Mouse learned so much and why he ultimately became such a good judge.

Trainer and contemporary amateur, Ted Walsh, remembers Mouse from around this time and is not shy about admitting that he probably had a bit more to offer than most amateurs of the day:

He was a very good amateur, very stylish – a good bit more stylish than I was or Timmy Jones – and he was very light too. I was more of an amateur, but he was more of a professional amateur. He was never going to be an 11st jockey and he was always able to do 10st or 9st 12lbs. He also rode a bit shorter than me, which he probably got from being over with Frenchie Nicholson, because he was riding out there with the flat lads like Eddery and Murray and he probably had a more professional way of riding as an amateur than any of the rest of us.

Tom Busteed of O'Grady's yard concurs:

In those days we got into racing by accident most of the time. Nowadays you expect children of jockeys and trainers to get involved and they get into it naturally. But Mouse was lucky, because Frenchie produced so many top jockeys it was a really good place to be. Frenchie not only trained horses, but he trained jockeys as well, and that was a great start for him. He developed a bit of style over there, but he would have had to develop quickly at Nicholson's. You either learned quickly or you got thrown out. And once he got to O'Grady's he had to have something, because there was nobody to guide you – to tell you how to sit on a horse, how to use your hands, all that stuff. He already had that when he got to Ballynonty [O'Grady's yard].

Mary O'Grady was – and still is – an integral part of the Ballynonty operation and she remembers a diminutive but well-bred young man who was 'fond of junk food – all that canned stuff, like beans and so on – but would never even look at something like bacon and cabbage.' Away from the kitchen table, however, she says Mouse had great respect for her husband and appreciated the trainer's authority in everything horse-related.

He lived in digs in Killenaule and, while Mrs O'Grady thought some of his traits were unusual for one so young – the flash cars and the unkempt demeanour – she always found him to be 'a most personable man'. Even so, she remembers that although it was fashionable at the time for men to have long hair, Willie would have none of it: 'Get your hair cut by the morning, or you won't be riding for me' was a refrain often heard around the yard.

She also remembers a guy who rode many winners, both for her husband and her son, and describes him as 'a good pilot'. She says her late husband always felt Mouse had great potential as a jockey, although she says Willie was never one for bandying plaudits around the place: 'He was just very pleased when it was a case of a job being well done. If it was not well done, then he was not so pleased.'

Her son, Edward, was still at college when Mouse arrived in Tipperary to work for his father and he recalls a shy, reserved young man with early indications of talent:

I would have known him from just knocking around in horsey circles. He was associated with Brian Cooper, whose daughter, Louise Cooper, I knew quite well. He came to us from England and I suppose that was because my father was very friendly with Frenchie Nicholson and generally in those days these things came about by word-of-mouth. You met someone at the races who knew somebody, who knew someone else and things just happened. He was very young when he appeared here and, like all young fellas, he was pretty vin de table when he started and he hated schooling horses. He was not very good at it and hated it, but on the track he was always very confident and he became a reasonably good professional jockey. He was as good in the afternoon as he was bad in the morning – which is the right way round really. It might not be satisfactory from a schooling point of view, but very satisfactory from a training point of view.

He had worked with the likes of Tony Murray and Pat Eddery when he was in England and he developed a flat-type crouch on a horse, as opposed to the more countryman's posture a lot of other National Hunt jockeys would have. I'd have to say that, because of his confidence on the track, horses did run for him. He was naturally very light and never had any problems with his weight …

Frank Berry, racing manager to the legendary punter, financier and philanthropist, J. P. McManus, and former Irish Champion Jockey, says he first met Mouse when he had just come back from Nicholson's and he saw him ride in a few point-to-points:

When he went to O'Grady's he progressed as an amateur very quickly and did very well and was always very stylish. He was a top-class jockey and was very neat. He was always part of the horse and looked the part when he got the leg-up. He always seemed to have the riding bug and it was something which he obviously loved doing.

★

Despite his otherwise shy demeanour, Mouse was quite a flashy character in those days, wearing the right clothes and driving the right cars. Having lived in digs for a while, he moved into a little lodge a few miles away from Ballynonty and was very much an independent entity, although there was nobody better than Willie O'Grady to make sure his feet were still firmly planted on the ground. Mouse had breakfast and lunch with the O'Gradys every day and Edward, like his mother, remembers him as a 'fussy grubber':

He'd only eat the breast of the chicken, for example, and it was not unknown for him to raid my mother's fridge. One story from back then had him arriving in one morning and asking my father if he would like to buy some lobster from him. Mouse had two cooked lobsters he'd got the night before in Galway or somewhere and he had them in the fridge. He had a love for lobster. My father said he'd love some lobster and Mouse said, 'I'll sell them to you.' My father was not impressed, thinking him to be a cheeky brat, but the matter was left at that.

Father had a very good friend staying with him at the time, a doctor from England called Nick English, and the two of them were chatting later in the morning and my father told him about the earlier incident. The doctor was a great prankster and he went to the fridge and took every ounce of meat out of the lobsters before putting them back in the bag they'd been in. When Mouse came in after evening stables he went to collect his lobster and noticed the bag was rather lighter than it had been. There was a girl working in the kitchen at the time and he accused her of stealing the meat, but she denied everything, as did the rest of the stable lads when he pointed the finger at them.

At that time of the day my father would have adjourned to his local hostelry in Killenaule and Mouse would have to pass there on the way home. Willie was there with Nick English when Mouse stomped in and accused them of stealing the lobster. They denied everything and Mouse went on his way still seething. That evening my father and his friend enjoyed a very pleasant lobster dinner and, at breakfast the next morning, Dr Nick couldn't contain himself and he said quietly across the table to my father, 'God Willie, that lobster was very good last night.' Mouse just about exploded. My mother didn't really feel that sorry for him though – on the basis of all the stuff he'd fecked out of her fridge here and there; she thought justice had been done.

Fussy eater aside, Ted Walsh says Mouse was managing to get over some of the class differences that might have arisen because of his status as the son of a lord:

> There was never any slagging over his background and I think that was down to the fact that Lord Killanin was such a widely respected man. I don't think there was anyone from any side of the fence who didn't respect him. The fact that Mouse was his son was irrelevant, really, and you have to remember that Lord Killanin was not in any way upper crust or stuffy. He was simply a very nice man. He was very much accepted by people as being an Irishman, despite the fact he was a lord. You were always made feel welcome when you went to visit the family home and his mother was a lovely woman too, very genteel. The thing about it is that his mother was a lady and his father was a gentleman, so unless he was a bastard he was going to turn out OK. Apples don't fall far from the tree.

Although not from the greater 'racing tribe', Ted Walsh reckons that it was not completely uncommon for a guy with Mouse's background to become a jockey:

> It happened occasionally in England where you got guys who were coming from well-to-do farming stock or whose father's background was in the City or something like that. A National Hunt jockey is a bit different from a flat jockey. National Hunt fellas

generally come from farming backgrounds or from families with lots of land, whereas flat jockeys are just lads who forgot to grow – no matter what background they came from.

The thing about Mouse was that he loved what he was doing and had always wanted to do it. He was a very good amateur and he eventually turned into a very good professional. He would probably have been a champion jockey one place or another at some stage if he hadn't had so many injuries. He got a lot of injuries as a professional and that sort of curtailed him making the grade at the real top level. You need a bit of luck in this game and he never had it. Unfortunately that was not in his control – you get broke up and there's nothing you can do about it.

Redmond Morris says this aspect of a jockey's life was something that concerned his parents but, while they were occasionally nervous for their son, they realised that injury was part of the deal:

Despite the fact my mother had been instrumental in Mouse becoming a jockey, she was always petrified when she went to the races to see him race. I remember going up to the National one year in Liverpool to see him ride and I remember he fell off the horse, but held on, remounted, and went on to finish the course. I suddenly realised at that point the sort of things he was going through on a daily basis. Anytime he'd break anything, you felt for him and you'd also feel for Mother too. But the family thinking at the time, I suppose, was that this was part of his job and if that's what it took for him to do the job, then so be it.

Former jockey, Tony Mullins, is a good friend and rival trainer. As a fully fledged member of the 'racing tribe', being the son of Paddy and brother to sibling trainers, Tom and Willie, he says that while a lot of people might only describe Mouse as an adequate jockey without class, you had to consider that he had no real background in racing and also that he had a late start:

He was very good for the foundation he had. I wouldn't have counted him as being really stylish, but he was quite a good jockey and his results were very good considering he really only rode for one stable which had two or three jockeys and only about forty horses. At that time a jockey's championship could be won with as little as forty-five winners and my memory of it is that he rode roughly thirty winners every year, so he was quite successful in the time that it was. If anything, being Lord Killanin's son could have impeded him as a jockey, but he didn't allow it to do so.

Ted Walsh and Edward O'Grady feel pretty much the same way. Ted says:

As a young fella, Mouse was probably a bit anti-establishment and he went to extremes at times to show people he was an ordinary Joe. The thing was that, to the rest of us, he *was* an ordinary Joe. But it seems like he had to go to extremes to prove it. He was a little bit rebellious to his background in that he only ever wore jeans and had long hair and was generally untidy, at a time when most of the rest of us wore a shirt and tie and sports coat. There was that hippy-ish look about him.

Whatever about the long hair and loud clothes, Edward O'Grady concurs that, as a person, Mouse was a gentleman – something he definitely inherited from his father – but that he was also quite rebellious:

Maybe it was that he just didn't want to be seen as his father's son. Everyone knew who he was, even though he tried desperately to be the opposite of what he was. If an ordinary guy was trying to get on he would not necessarily have behaved in the same way Mouse did. An ordinary guy would strive to improve his way of life, whereas Mouse seemed to have a death wish, not so much to 'disimprove' his life, but he certainly engaged in a different sort of life than you might have anticipated with someone of his background. If you thought he'd do something a particular way, then the odds usually were that he'd do it another way. You certainly wouldn't set your clock by him.

He was a very extrovert character and while on the one side he wanted to act and talk like a stable lad, he also liked the finer things – the souped-up cars and the Carnaby Street clothes. I'd suppose you'd have to say he was a complex character.

Lifelong friend and jeweller to the racing fraternity, Mattie Ryan, recalls a man who was 'the Ruby Walsh of his day', because he was very poised on a horse and never moved his hands, riding 'with great courage into fences'.

It is probably fair to say that while Mouse had a great relationship with Willie O'Grady – something which Mattie Ryan also stresses – the same was never true of himself and Edward, even though the two will sometimes these days admit to having had successful and happy times together. 'When Timmy Hyde retired as stable jockey I turned professional and took over from him,' Mouse says. 'I had won the four-mile chase [the National Hunt Chase] in 1974 for Edward on Mr Midland, which was his first victory there, and it was after that I turned professional. We had some great successes,' Mouse admits.

O'Grady himself recalls that win and gives Mouse due credit:

> He rode my first Cheltenham winner and I remember Mr Midland was not a very easy horse to ride because he had a tendency to fall or make very bad mistakes. He also tended to keep a bit back in his races. It was a very good renewal of the race that year. Chris Collins rode a horse called Cricket Call in it and he won the Pardubice [steeplechase] on him afterwards. But the horse ran really well for Mouse and he produced him to perfection to win really well.

That victory on Mr Midland in the so-called 'amateurs' Grand National' persuaded Mouse it was time to join the professional ranks. Tom Busteed would take over from Mouse as the stable amateur when Timmy Hyde retired and Tom remembers learning a riding trick or two from the new professional in the yard:

> Mouse had his own style: he was very neat on a horse. He always had his irons twisted so he only had his foot in the corner of the stirrup, but he never looked cumbersome. Any pictures you'd see of him he was always very tidy. I always thought he was a very underrated pilot. At the time he was riding for Edward, he had a lot of good horses and there were about sixty of them in the yard and the stable was doing very well. There were plenty of fancied horses for Mouse to ride and from my point of view there were a lot of Bumper horses too. Edward was always a fair man to train for Cheltenham and I'd

say that's where Mouse got the taste for the Festival. The early horses he would have ridden there included Kilmacillogue and Golden Lancer and he won plenty of big races on them.

Big races aside, humour was never far from the surface and Mouse was a somewhat mischievous character at the best of times: O'Grady himself recalls an incident at Sandown with a horse called Kublai which, curiously, never won a race for him in Ireland, despite multiple successes with Mouse aboard in both France and England.

On one occasion the horse ran twice on consecutive days in England at Sandown's Grand Military meeting. On the Friday he won with Mouse up and the connections were well pleased with the effort and were enjoying a few glasses of champagne.

However, Kublai was also entered for a 'Past and Present' race the following day and the trainer was under the impression that the only qualification for the race was that the owner should be a past or present member of the armed forces in the UK. Since the horse's owner, Desmond Browne, had served in the British Army, O'Grady presumed that the qualification was fulfilled. But he hadn't realised that there was a second rule: only jockeys who had served the Queen in the military could ride and the overnight declaration had seen Mouse down to ride the horse again. In O'Grady's words:

I remember there was an announcement over the Tannoy to the effect that would Messrs O'Grady and Morris report to the Stewards Room. I couldn't understand what was going on, as I did not know what I was supposed to have done that merited being brought before the Stewards. Anyway, we went in and, with it being the Grand Military meeting, the Stewards were all particularly military men – Major General This and Brigadier That: very nice gentlemen, but very much army-orientated. I don't recall who the Chief Steward was, but he said to me, 'Mr O'Grady, I understand Kublai is due to run again tomorrow.' I said this was the case, but he then asked who I intended to ride the horse. I said that Mr Morris was the intended rider. The Steward then said: 'Morris, this race is confined to people who have been in the forces – past or present. Have you ever been in the army?' To which Mouse replied, 'No sir, only the IRA, sir.'

Give them their dues, the gentlemen got a real belly laugh out of that. They got a great kick out of it, but the response from the Chief Steward, when the laughing died down, was, 'I'm afraid, Morris, that just won't do.' Thankfully things were not as bad in the north of Ireland as they subsequently became and I was grateful we didn't get involved in a Steward's Inquiry, because I don't think we'd have won one. A guy called Major Bobby Faulkner won on him the next day, but Mouse was out of luck in the Imperial Cup when Judy Cullen led over the last, but was run down at the finish, so it wasn't his lucky day.

★

Ironically, Mouse's biggest successes in the professional ranks did not come from the O'Grady yard, but rather from somewhere that was not so prominent on the racing map. Back in the mid-1970s there was a thriving racing scene in Northern Ireland and one of its leading lights was trainer Brian Lusk, for whom Mouse turned out to a very lucky jockey. Lusk remembers:

> He rode a good number of winners for me over a three or four year period, the most obvious being the success of Skymas in the Champion Chase in 1976 and 1977. I was only in the game for about ten years and I have to say it was quite a successful time and obviously Skymas was the most successful horse we had. A farmer beside me at the time bred him and when he was five he was wrong of his wind and had to be hobdayed and he didn't actually run until he was a six-year-old.
>
> He was a bit of an old boy to ride at the start, because when he was on a left-hand track he hung to the right and when he was on a right-hand track he hung to the left. I remember Dermot Weld rode in him a Bumper at Leopardstown for six-year-olds and upwards and when he got off he said, 'It'll be a slow race he'll win.'
>
> Skymas never actually fell, you know – even when he was a novice. He always showed improvement and although he was a puller and always wanted to make the running and also tended to hang when under pressure, these were things he grew out of. He was a nine-year-old by the time he came to his best.

Frank Berry actually rode Skymas the first time he appeared at Cheltenham, although he did not win on that occasion:

> I'd ridden the horse the year before Mouse won the Champion Chase on him in 1976 and he ran a blinder in the 1975 race to finish third behind Royal Relief. The following year Mouse took up the job with Brian Lusk and he had a lot of winners for him, as well as winning the two Champion Chases on Skymas in 1976 and 1977. I had the opportunity to take the job that year, but I had other commitments and it was just one of those things. Skymas himself was very underrated and he was a much better horse than he was ever credited with. He'd won the Mackeson before Mouse or I ever rode him and he was one of a big team that Brian had at the time.
>
> For a few years he did very well and at that time the North was a real hotbed for National Hunt racing. There were a lot of big punters up there and they really liked their racing. He [Lusk] had the support of a lot of big businessmen and he had sixty or seventy horses on the go up there. Skymas was the star turn there, though, and he won a lot of races apart from the Champion Chase victories. I won two big chases on him up in Ayr and he was also third in the Irish National as well a lot of other big races.
>
> He was actually a big, heavy-headed horse and he could take off with you if you let him. He used always make the running in his early days, but as he got older he lost form and we tried holding him up more and that worked well because he got a new lease of life being held up. The third place in the Irish National was interesting because it was way beyond his normal trip, but he just had the class to do it.

Some might not recall Skymas as the classy animal Berry remembers but, with two Champion Chases under his belt, a Mackeson Gold Cup, four wins in handicap chases at Punchestown and a victory over the great Tingle Creek in the Sandown race which is now named after the legendary two-mile champion, the indications are that he was a lot better than some thought at the time. Brian Lusk certainly still has fond memories:

> The first time he ran in the Champion Chase, Frank Berry rode him and he was half-left at the start but still managed to finish third.

He then won it the next two years with Mouse on board. Mouse had turned professional when I started to give him a few rides and things just developed from there. He was the number one jockey at O'Grady's but he was riding for me when he was available. He also won the Kerry National on a horse called Black Mac for me.

Mouse was a top-class rider, no doubt about that … He had great balance and he was well able to ride a finish. He rode Skymas in the run-up to the Champion Chase in 1976 and we were quite confident going over there. He was a real good top-of-the-ground horse and that year the ground was spot on for him, even though the following year it was quite soft, but he won it again.

We'd been quite confident going there again the second year, but the weather was bad and the closer we got to the race the less the confidence got. Mouse really clicked with the horse, of that there is no doubt. He knew the old horse inside out. It was ironic in many ways that in 1977, when we won the Champion Chase, that not only was Mouse's riding career going to end shortly after that, but also my career as a trainer and the horse's racing career.

Mouse also rode him to win the Sun Rating Chase, a limited handicap, and I still have a picture on the wall of my office with Mouse and himself jumping the water jump at Aintree. Skymas never, ever had a problem – never took a lame step – but when he was eleven he was out in a field having a break in the summertime and he split his pastern. We got him back and tried him out in a hurdle, but it went again at the last hurdle in that race and that was the end of him.

Recalling the end of his own training career at the same time, Lusk says, 'What fucked it up back in 1978, or thereabouts, was the Irish punt coming into being.' When the punt was established it was worth 25 per cent less than the pound sterling, and there was also a 15 per cent VAT charge in Northern Ireland on training fees, so the whole training game was no longer feasible. The punt, Lusk feels, largely killed racing in Northern Ireland:

The thing was that, apart from the racing at the Maze and Downpatrick, you were racing for prize money in punts, so it became economically untenable. Archie Watson, Leslie Crawford and myself were the main guys training in the North at the time, but we all stopped. I supposed we could have moved south to train, but that was not really a runner. There's nobody really doing it now in the North – or very few at least.

I jacked it in then and I moved to England a year later and I started off a business where I buy and sell horses, mainly for National Hunt racing and for eventing as well. I always buy a couple of National Hunt foals every year and then sell them off at the Derby Sale when they are three. But I remember those days well and winning two Champion Chases with Mouse and Skymas is something that will always be with me. It was an amazing coincidence that our three careers ended almost simultaneously.

The same year was to see Mouse win the Irish Grand National on the Adrian Maxwell-trained Billycan (the same race that precipitated his father's heart attack), but the tragedy of the Colonial Cup came only months later. Liam Burke, stalwart of Mouse's Everardsgrange yard in County Tipperary and ex-head lad, remembers that 'he snapped an arm one day in a race without even falling.'

Although his professional career was relatively short, Mouse still contrived to finish second and third in the Jockey's Championship in the course of it and Frank Berry feels he was terribly unlucky that his career was cut short so early:

> The year he broke his leg in America, he was going really well in the Jockey's Championship here and, if I remember correctly, there was only a couple of winners between us when that happened. He was going really well at the time and it was very unfortunate that it took him so long to get back and even then he was not a hundred per cent. It is a funny game at the best of times but Mouse was very unlucky because he never really got a run at it with all the injuries he got. He did have a lot of success, but his career was always being interrupted with different breaks and knocks.
>
> Had he had a bit more luck he could have gone back to Cheltenham for four or five more years but it never happened for him that way and his bad luck was good news for the likes of Boots Madden and Tommy Ryan who rode a good few winners for O'Grady at Cheltenham after he had to retire.

Edward O'Grady believes that, 'It was probably very unfortunate he broke his leg about the time I hit into rich vein of good horses. Golden Cygnet came along in 1978, the year after his Colonial Cup accident, and it was probably cruel in terms of his career. He did come back after he broke his leg, but things were never quite the same again for him.' Mouse confirms as much:

> I remember O'Grady giving me a pep talk on the way to Naas one day when I'd given one of his horses a wicked ride a few days previously. I'd had a fall at Navan three days earlier and my arm was very sore, despite being checked out in hospital. But I was upsides in the lead going to the last and giving the horse holly, but the arm just snapped while I was jumping the fence. I now understand what people mean when they talk about phantom limbs – I thought my hand was on the reins, but it was actually around by my back. I was off to hospital again. That was it really.

In spite of his injury concerns, Mouse was a bit of a thrill-seeker and his twin brother John recalls that even when the two were at school, Mouse was always looking for something to get the adrenaline flowing:

> He was always something of a daredevil – always up to something and afraid of nothing. I was quite nervous and I remember times when we had to fly back to school in England and I'd be terrified and he'd be laughing his head off. He had nerves of steel. I remember when he came back to Ireland after breaking his leg in America that time [the Colonial Cup] that he went hang-gliding with his leg in plaster. At the time people were saying that he'd lost his nerve, but you don't go hang-gliding with your leg in plaster if your nerve is gone. It was out on Achill Island, I remember, and I was in the horrors watching him.

Ex-wife Shanny (née Clarke) also recalls a man for whom personal danger held little meaning:

> When I first met him, one of the things that attracted and interested me was the fact that he used to go canoeing and hang-gliding and things like that. I remember his hang-glider was so big it took two

of us to carry it up to the top of the Sugarloaf. I'd carry it up to the top of the mountain with him, set it up, wave him off, and have to run down to the bottom while he floated down. And then I'd help him do it again. How mad was I? Needless to say, that was before we got married.

He lived for the hunting too. While he loved the horses and the hounds, I think it was just the madness of it all that really appealed to him. He wasn't very well-disciplined and he used to do his own thing and go off in front.

Carol Swan (née Hyde) has known Mouse for many years, initially through his association with her father and as a family friend. Amongst her most vivid memories of Mouse away from the track are those involving various pursuits – each one more dangerous than the last:

Myself and Mouse were out one day on a speedboat my Dad owned in Killaloe. I was driving the boat and he is a very good water-skier. I was whizzing along in the boat and he was flying along behind on just one ski and he kept shouting at me to keep in towards the bank because he was showing off and trying to pick bits of grass off the bank. The next thing I remember was that there was a big crash and the boat was completely written off. There were rocks in the water close to the bank and we hit them and that was the end of the boat.

Those daredevil days were coming to an end, in the same way as was Mouse's riding career. It was time now to concentrate on a closely associated but very different life.

5   Gay Future

'Peer's Son Named In Race Scandal' screamed the front-page headline in the *Irish Independent* of 3 June 1975. In typical 'shock–horror' style, the coverage told readers that 'the jockey son of Olympic supremo, Lord Killanin, is wanted by Scotland Yard in the Gay Future betting coup case.' The paper went on to say that a warrant had been granted to Detective Chief Superintendent Terence O'Connell at Ulverston Magistrates' Court in Cumbria, and that this would now have to be executed by the Gardaí in Ireland.

Further, the *Irish Independent* story revealed that Mouse was one of eight Irishmen to be named in connection with the coup which was pulled off 'at the tiny Cartmel course' the previous August: 'Already, his boss, trainer Eddie O'Grady, Cork businessmen Brian Darrer, Tony Murphy and John Horgan have been charged and remanded in connection with the coup. But last month three other Corkmen, including a Garda superintendent, successfully fought a Scotland Yard extradition warrant linking them with the coup.'

This was a story which was picked up not only by all the Irish papers, but also – because of Lord Killanin's status as President of the IOC – attracted interest from the British dailies, not least the *Daily Telegraph* and the *Daily Mirror*, the latter noting that Mouse had ridden a winner at Tramore the day the warrant was issued in England. 'When told last night that a warrant had been issued for his arrest, he exclaimed: "What, me? It's the first news I have had about it",' the *Mirror* reported.

In horse-racing history the so-called 'Gay Future affair' has gained legendary status as a wonderful example of smart Irish punters taking on the big British bookmakers and beating them, only to be foiled by the combined might of the establishment in Britain who could not possibly countenance being taken to the cleaners by a bunch of upstart Paddies.

That the coup subsequently spawned books, a television movie and countless newspaper columns in Ireland and Britain – not to mention endless hours of debate among racing people and punters – is an indication of the almost mythical status the case has attained. Funnily enough, there have been innumerable examples of similar coup attempts, but none has gained the same notoriety. Tom Busteed, Edward O'Grady's amateur at the time, remembers one or two similar cases:

> Those sorts of things went on all the time – those off-course gambles. Barney Curley famously ran one in Bellewstown when Yellow Sam pulled off a massive coup. It was the same as the Gay Future thing almost to a tee – no blower at the course, all the money laid down in bookie shops.
>
> Another involved my late wife, Avril, who was quite a good jockey and I remember she got a call from John Hassett to ride a horse of his in a Ladies' Bumper at the Phoenix Park one day. She'd been anaemic and was run down totally and explained this to him but he just said, 'You'll be fit enough.' She got a lift to the Park on the day, got changed and arrived into the paddock only to find there was no trainer there. There was only a lad there to leg her up. The horse was a big mare called Humble Pickings, but Avril hadn't a clue what was going on. The horse was 50/1 and there she was going out having had no instructions.
>
> At the Park in those days, you left the parade ring and went out past this hedge and you're straight out onto the track. As Avril passed the hedge, Hassett suddenly stuck his head out and told her to jump off and stick with the leaders. He said that she was to be handy coming into the final bend and not to hit the horse with the whip. 'Don't hit her and just keep her balanced – she'll give you everything.' She won by a head and they cleaned up. Apparently they backed the horse in the shops in Scotland and to this day it is untold what money they made out of it. It was a massive gamble, but yet the biggest single bet was no more than £50.

Two of those involved in the Gay Future affair (Tony Murphy and Tony Collins) were later tried and convicted at Preston Crown Court of 'conspiring to defraud bookmakers by attempting to win by means of fraud and ill-practice multiple and single wager bets made by them or on their behalf on 26 August 1974, on horses named Gay Future, Ankerwyke and Opera Cloak, contrary to common law'. However the widely accepted bottom line is that, hiding behind a thin veneer of respectability, British bookmakers avoided having to make a pay-out of over £200,000 (estimated to be worth about £5 million today) and the Irish gamblers were done out of a rightful pay-day.

★

The coup was organised by garrulous Cork businessman and builder, Tony Murphy – a Rolls-Royce owner at a time when such luxury was almost completely unheard-of in Ireland. He and his cohorts persuaded Edward O'Grady to find and train a horse for them that could be used for another tilt at a whopping off-course gamble to take advantage of the British bookmaking system, which allowed multiple double and treble bets to funnel onto one single horse in the event of the others being non-runners.

The plan was to place these multiple bets in such a way that when the two no-hopers were withdrawn from their intended races, three-quarters of the money would then lump on to the certainty, which in this case was Gay Future. Although Gay Future was, in reality, trained by O'Grady in Ireland, he was nominally registered as being in the care of stockbroker and part-time trainer, Tony Collins, at his yard near Troon in Scotland. He also trained Ankerwyke and Opera Cloak.

On that fateful August bank holiday Monday, Gay Future was entered in the Ulverston Novices' Hurdle at Cartmel, while Ankerwyke and Opera Cloak were entered in races at Plumpton and Southwell. Apart from being an isolated rural track, Cartmel suited the needs of the Irish gamblers because it was not equipped with a 'blower' – a telephone link used by bookies at most courses to relay off-course bets back to the track to compress starting prices to suit themselves. This, and the fact that there was only one public phone – easily engaged to prevent high-street bookmakers contacting their course representatives to lower the starting price of any horse on which they had major potential liabilities – made the course ideal for the coup's perpetrators.

Gathering all the essential parts – buying a horse, securing two enthusiastic trainers, selecting the right venue and a team of people to manage the various other disparate elements of the coup – was not actually as difficult as it might seem. However John Horgan, one of the central figures involved in the planning and execution of the coup, remembers only too well that the effort had to be very carefully orchestrated. He recalls that the horse was bought from Johnny Harrington (husband of trainer Jessica) after the Punchestown Festival in April 1974: 'He had been ridden there by Hugo de Burgh and was beaten when he should have won, but we bought him anyway and he was then laid out for what would happen the following August.'

O'Grady was finding his feet as a trainer at the time, after taking over his father's yard which he ran as what was then called a 'gambling yard'. Horgan says of O'Grady, 'I don't think it took too much persuasion. He just felt – like the rest of us – that the system could be bucked. As well as that, he was young and there was an element of fearlessness there too.'

Mouse admits he did most of the preparatory work with Gay Future but he insists that if anyone had been watching carefully enough before Cartmel they would have spotted this was a decent horse:

> He had won previously for Richard Annsley before we bought him and his form was there for anyone to see and that form wasn't bad at all. But, from the time we bought him, he was not seen on a racecourse until he was sent to Cartmel.
>
> He was sent over a few days before and the whole thing should have gone off without a hitch, but there was a major fuck-up because Tony Collins never sent Ankerwyke and Opera Cloak to their intended destinations.

Some months before Cartmel there had been another off-course coup attempt, when O'Grady ran a horse called Golden Lancer in Scotland. The horse ran at Ayr on Easter Monday 1974 with the idea of raising a few bob to fund the real thing, but he fell and there was nothing made of it at the time. Mouse says: 'It was the same thing because he was doubled up with another horse that did not run, but because he fell and didn't win there wasn't a peep about it. The bookies kept the money that day and they weren't complaining.'

Golden Lancer's owner was Brian Darrer who played a very active role in Gay Future's subsequent win at Cartmel, since it was he who

artfully commandeered the only public phone at the track so that the
bookies could not phone their respective head offices. Tom Busteed
recalls the run-up to Cartmel, which also involved Golden Lancer:

> Edward was a shrewd guy and he always had a great head on him
> and I remember one day we were brought to the Curragh – myself
> and Pat Hanley, who was a great work rider and jockey, as well as
> Mouse and Timmy Jones. We had four horses: one was called Storm
> Damage and the other was called Goldings and they were both very
> average horses; we also had Gay Future and Golden Lancer. Being
> honest about it, I'd say we were oblivious to what was going on
> and what was being planned. Pat and myself schooled the first two
> and I fell from mine and, to be honest, I was relieved because I was
> dreading the next fence every time. When we were finished, Mouse
> was sent out on Golden Lancer and Timmy Jones was put up on
> Gay Future.
>
> Golden Lancer was a really good horse and had won on the flat
> as well as over hurdles and fences – very versatile. He even won a
> Cesarewich. Anyway, the two of them worked over a mile and a
> half, stride for stride. That was midweek and I remember the
> following weekend [before the Cartmel coup on the bank holiday
> Monday], when I was in charge for a few days for some reason, that
> when I arrived in on the Saturday morning the lorry was gone, the
> saddle was gone, the bridle was gone, the head lad, Tim Finn, was
> gone and so was the horse. Most lads wouldn't even think twice
> about such a thing, but the whole affair was so cloak-and-dagger
> that I was left wondering what was going on.

★

The Irish cabal, including Murphy, John Horgan, Mouse and many
more, assembled in London the night before the race and the following
morning they set out with large amounts of cash to put down their
double and treble bets. Mouse remembers each team of betters being
issued with money and instructions before they went into battle. Mouse
was paired with his elder brother, Redmond, who was following a
London-based career in film at the time and was happy to give a hand
on an otherwise boring bank holiday Monday. As Mouse says:

We were laying bets down in London. My brother was driving –
he was living in London at the time. Tony Murphy was a good
man and I'd ridden winners for him at O'Grady's. But he was way
ahead of his time even to come up with a scheme like this. The
planning that went into this was almost ridiculous. We had maps
of London handed out to us with all the bookies' shops marked
out. We were even given the *A-to-Z* of London so we could find
our way around.

But Jesus, we visited some places I can tell you. There were
places where I was the only white man in the shop. The first place
I went to was down in the East End – where the whole Docklands
development now is. It was early in the morning and the man in
the first bookie's we went to asked me if I was off a ship and I was
there pretending I was deaf and dumb. I remember one place in
Wandsworth – near the prison – and they must have got wind of
what was going on at that stage because the manager came
running out of the shop after me and chased us down the road as
we drove off.

There must have been at least ten cars driving around London
that day with fellas in them placing bets all over the place. That
was why the Special Branch initially thought we were the IRA.
Tony Murphy had taken a large chunk of money out of the bank
and in those days the banks had to report any large or suspicious
transactions and apparently we were followed around the place
until they realised what we were up to and they buggered off.

Redmond himself recalls that he did not really have a clue what was
going on and it was not until some time later he realised just how big
this thing was:

We were all over London and I remember there was money
spread all over the floor of the car. I knew there was something
going on – some kind of skulduggery – so I can't claim complete
ignorance. I was actually doing a movie at the time ... and all the
extras were well into the horses. When the thing hit the headlines
the next day, I so wanted to be able to tell them that I was
involved, but I couldn't.

With the money down in large volumes, albeit in very many small bets so as not to arouse suspicion, it was not until late in the day that the bookies collectively realised they had a very large potential liability going on Gay Future in the 4.20 at Cartmel. They tried to contact the course to shorten his starting price, but Brian Darrer was actively engaged on the sole public telephone at Cartmel, so they just had to sit back and see what happened.

Gay Future duly won at 10/1 by fifteen lengths, ridden by Timmy Jones, whose comical antics in the parade ring beforehand were aimed at persuading local punters that the horse had no chance.

Everything seemed to have clicked and Murphy and his cohorts appeared to have pulled off the coup they had dreamed of. Wild celebrations at their base at the Tara Hotel in Kensington ensued.

Back in Ireland there had been bank holiday racing in Tramore and Tom Busteed recalls riding there for O'Grady on a horse called Golden Express, which was owned by Mick Cuddy:

> He was actually fairly useless and only ended up third or fourth. I had no inkling what was going on across in England and the first time I got a glimmer of what might be happening was after my race when Edward told me to get changed and go out to the car and listen to the radio for the results from Cartmel. It was then that it clicked with me.
>
> When I came back in and told him that Gay Future had won at 10/1, he told me to drive him to the home of a great owner of his called Major Cunningham, which was nearby. He was a great character and he actually owned a mare that Mouse rode on several occasions called Judy Cullen, who was named after Edward's wife back then – her maiden name was Cullen.
>
> Anyway the two of them stayed up until the early hours drinking champagne and I drove Edward home after that. A few days later all hell broke loose.

The initial celebrations were not confined to Waterford and back in London the party was in full swing. 'On the day we thought we had pulled it off', Mouse says, 'we all gathered back at the Tara Hotel. We were all there getting mogalorum when someone came in and said there was a problem getting paid – that the bookies were refusing to pay out.'

The fly in the ointment, as it transpired, was that Collins had never sent either Ankerwyke or Opera Cloak to their respective engagements and had left them at home in Troon. Murphy's instructions to him had been to send them on their way to the tracks where they were supposed to appear but then organise some problem with their transport so they could not reach their intended destinations. Collins did not follow the plan and, when Jockey Club inquiries discovered neither horse had left Troon, the bookies had the excuse they were looking for, cried foul and demanded a police investigation.

Lord Wigg, the Chairman of the Bookmakers Association in the UK and the person upon whose shoulders the Irish laid much of the blame for what subsequently happened, was to the fore in demanding official action. He soon got it in spades, as a major police investigation began.

That investigation came to a head at the opening day of the Cheltenham Festival the following year, on 10 March 1975 to be exact, when detectives led by Detective Chief Superintendent O'Connell raided the famous Queens Hotel in the town and arrested O'Grady, Darrer, Murphy and Horgan. Unsurprisingly the experience has left a mark on John Horgan to this day:

> I'd been on the piss all night the previous night and then the police arrived early in the morning and we were bundled into cars and taken to the police station in Cheltenham. We got no breakfast or anything – not even a cup of tea. After that, myself, O'Grady, Darrer and Murphy were driven at high speed up the motorway to Kendal where we were thrown into a jail.
>
> The next morning we were brought before these judges [magistrates] and we were remanded and as we were being led away I remember one of the cops asking O'Grady if he fancied anything in the 3.20 at Cheltenham that day. You can imagine the answer he got.
>
> We were bailed for big money and I remember having to ring home to try and get cash over to England. They wouldn't take a personal surety from any of us, so I had to get a brother of mine who lived in England to go into his local police station and sign for the bail. Tony Murphy had to get some building pal of his from Manchester to do the same for him. They really went to town on

us. It was as if we were after blowing up half of England. Times were very different then, especially for Irishmen in England.

Mattie Ryan remembers that day well and recalls that after the police descended on Horgan and Murphy he ran to warn Gay Future's jockey, Timmy Jones. Jones promptly climbed out the window of his hotel, shinned down a drainpipe and took off for Paris, from where he was able to get a direct flight back to Dublin.

The afternoon they were released, they hired a helicopter to fly them back to Cheltenham for the rest of the racing, but for O'Grady and Darrer there was further heartbreak when Golden Lancer was a well-beaten favourite and it seemed the trip was becoming a nightmare.

And for Mouse, it was about to get worse. Everything seemingly calmed down after Cheltenham – the four Irishmen were awaiting a trial date and the Irish had returned home in their droves, with the Gay Future crew in particular only too delighted to be getting the hell out of there – but then in June a warrant was issued for Mouse's arrest.

He was quoted in the papers as saying he was 'completely shocked by this turn of events'. His father was also quoted when news of the warrant emerged: 'I know nothing about the warrant other than what I heard on the news,' he said, adding, in typically steadfast and understated fashion, 'I have not been in touch with my son today and as far as I know he is scheduled to ride at Sligo tomorrow.'

Lord Killanin, by then President of the IOC, was privately more than a little worried by the chain of events. He happened to meet Terence O'Connell in the Turf Club one day and the British policeman assured him that his son would ultimately not be charged with anything and that he should not be concerned.

Mouse initially thought he was in the clear and that the whole business of the warrant would be quietly shelved. It was not to be. He now reckons that he was 'implicated only because they were running out of options'. Even so, this led to a fairly hairy experience for him when returning from Cheltenham a year later in 1976:

> Once I knew the British police had issued a warrant, I got a solicitor to write to them saying that we would meet them where and whenever they wanted. I had nothing to hide at all and, after we wrote to them, they withdrew the warrant.

I had travelled to Cheltenham with no concerns about anything, but I'd just boarded an Aer Lingus flight to come home when the pilot announced there was a problem and we had to return to the terminal. When we got back, there was an announcement requesting that 'Mr Morris make himself known to the crew', and I was then removed from the flight by three burly policemen. I was marched off and locked up in a room for a while. I told them my story and they went off to check it out and it transpired the warrant had been removed and I was told I was free to go. When I was arrested it was only because the detective in question wanted headlines – they were grasping at straws at that stage. I seem to remember I hired a private plane to fly home – I couldn't get out of there quick enough.

John Horgan, who was travelling home on the same flight, has a slightly different memory of the incident in that he recalls his brother, Jim, getting off the Aer Lingus flight with Mouse while he and the rest of the travelling party continued on to Dublin: 'We told them to ring us at the Gresham [Hotel] when there was news and I remember Jim ringing to say that the police realised it was a mistake and were apologising and everything. They got the next plane back.'

Both men are agreed, however, as to where the blame lay for turning what was, ostensibly, a fairly simple coup attempt – one oft previously and subsequently attempted, according to Cork bookmaker Liam Cashman – into a major conspiracy.

'Only for Lord Wigg', Mouse says, 'we would have got paid. He was in the bookies' pocket because he was head of the Bookmakers Association and there was this anti-Irish feeling abroad, but he was the fly in the ointment. Apparently he owed the bookies a lot of money.'

Liam Cashman is in no doubt that the whole effort to prosecute the Irish cabal was 'highly political' and he maintains that Irish bookies 'wouldn't even dream' of doing what their British counterparts did: 'If an Irish bookie tried not to pay out for something like that, they'd be out of business in double-quick time, because nobody would give them any business.'

He remembers another coup around the same time, involving a horse called Adorable Princess that won at 33/1 in Downpatrick, and which also involved non-runners, cleaning the bookies out. But, he says,

'There was not a murmur from the bookmakers because they could not afford to squeal. They had to swallow it.' John Horgan is much of the same mind:

> The Gay Future thing turned into a major schemozzle because Lord Wigg made it out that a major fraud had been committed. The thing was that everyone in racing thought different because nothing would have happened if the horse lost. They all saw it for what it was – a gamble. But he turned it into something else and of course it went forward to the courts.

He cites the fact that, of all those questioned and charged, only two – Murphy and Collins – were ever put into the dock and tried, although himself and O'Grady were also initially in the dock at Preston Crown Court before being stood down when the prosecution offered no evidence against them. Horgan says:

> The whole thing was taken all out of proportion, but I suppose in the mid-seventies things were not good in terms of Anglo-Irish relations, what with the Birmingham and Guildford bombings and so on. I was actually returned for trial and was in the dock at the outset of the trial and I remember the judge asking, 'What are they doing there?' when the prosecution offered 'no prosecution against O'Grady and Horgan', and then being instructed to leave the dock.

Horgan does not think that the British police were particularly on top of their brief when it came to the whole matter and, to illustrate his point, he highlights the fact that they tried to extradite several alleged conspirators – including the late Chief Superintendent Seamus McMahon who was then based at Union Quay in Cork – on charges which existed in British law but were not on the Irish statute books:

> Even in court [at an earlier extradition hearing in Dublin] they did not make a great case and I remember a Garda saying to me, 'This is a load of shit, the judge will throw this out in ten minutes' – which he did. Terry O'Connell was the Scotland Yard man in Dublin that day and I remember him ranting and raving that this was 'disgraceful justice' but I told him to wake up and think what

would happen if the shoe was on the other foot and Irish police were in England trying to extradite British people on the basis of a cock-and-bull story. I met him years later, when he was head of security at Ascot, so he didn't do too badly in the end.

He admits the fact that Collins 'didn't do what he was told' gave the British establishment the peg on which to hang a conspiracy trial. 'It was a stupid thing he did, but these things happen,' he says with a world-weary sigh, continuing:

> The motivating force was nothing other than a bit of fun trying to land a gamble. We were just trying to take advantage of how the SP [starting price] system worked in England. We were only working that system and we'd tried it before and it didn't come off. The thing was that the horse had to win and he did. In my book that makes it a gamble.
>
> The other thing you have to remember when it comes to gambles like this is that the telephone systems in those days were prehistoric and that really helped, particularly when it came to off-course gambles.

Horgan reckons that some English bookies were appalled by the fact that many of their counterparts were refusing to pay out and he says that one who did cough up even volunteered to go to court to give evidence as to why he had paid out: 'A few of them paid out, but the majority of them hid behind the conspiracy thing. And, of course, if the trial had failed then we could have gone back and got everything, but when Murphy and Collins were found guilty, that was the end of that.'

In the heel of the hunt, Mouse himself has strong personal feelings on what happened in the Preston courtroom that day:

> Personally I believe that the bookies got at the jury. I've no doubt they were tampered with. I mean, they were instructed by the judge to acquit and they didn't. And the other thing you have to remember is that all this was going on at the same time as stuff like the Birmingham bombing and the general view of the Irish over there was black to say the least – that clouded everything. But the thing was that when you read the judge's summing up, there had to

be something rinky-dink about the finding the jury arrived at. Also, the fact that even after the boys were found guilty the judge only gave them the absolute minimum penalty he could under the law showed what he thought of their decision.

John Horgan is not so sure the jury was got at but he feels that they were certainly of an age profile that did not suit the alleged conspirators: 'There were a few elderly women on the jury and you could see they had their minds made up before it even started.'

At the end of the day, the Irish recouped nothing near the sum that they should have and Mouse reckons that whatever proceeds were collected from those bookies that paid out were eventually soaked up by the legal fees incurred by Murphy and his associates. 'The night we had in the Tara Hotel was about the only benefit we got out of it in the end. We had a lot of champagne,' he reflects.

Mouse also admits that, like many of the others of those involved – Edward O'Grady in particular ('I know nothing about that' is a fairly standard response when the Gay Future topic is raised) – he tried to forget it had ever happened. He confesses that for many years afterwards he denied he had anything to do with the affair at all, especially when his two boys were growing up: 'I was afraid they'd get into trouble at school or something but, as it transpired, the two of them were delighted to eventually find out that I'd been in the thick of it. They even gave me a present of the *Murphy's Stroke* video for Christmas one year!'

For John Horgan and others though, there are no regrets at having been involved in one of the most infamous racing scandals of all time. He says pointedly:

The only regret we had was getting messed around afterwards, which was not very pleasant. It was not nice having your name dragged through the mud by heavy-handed British authorities. The fact that no case was brought against myself and O'Grady in the heel of the hunt showed that we never really had a case to answer and it is my firm belief that if Tony Murphy hadn't been so vocal in the press, he'd have got off too. He was labelled as a 'mastermind' in the papers and that went against him in the end.

Collins and Murphy were eventually fined £1,000 each, with £500 costs after the jury ignored Mr Justice Caulfield's directions and decided they were guilty as charged. Both were also subsequently warned off by the Jockey Club for ten years. Many regarded the outcome as a complete miscarriage of justice but the central characters were just relieved it was all over and they immediately set about putting the affair behind them and getting on with their lives. Unfortunately, such is the infamy of the case, they may never be able to do that.

★

There is one ironic footnote to the whole story, concerning Redmond Morris' involvement in the coup. He was subsequently asked to get involved with the production of the television version of the story, which ultimately became *Murphy's Stroke*. Redmond's connections with the Gay Future coup were unknown to those who offered him the job, but he decided to give it a miss anyway. 'He was busy,' Mouse recalls.

Redmond remembers the *Murphy's Stroke* director, Frank Citanovic, who was then married to Janet Street-Porter, ringing him at home in Kew and asking him to get involved: 'I was actually an assistant director at the time and when Frank outlined the story to me, I said to him, "Frank do you want me as an assistant director or a technical adviser?" He quickly put two and two together.'

6   Early Training

As Mouse started into his training career, the initial portents may not have seemed favourable for he had no money and no owners, but he had his admirers from the outset. Compliments from rival trainers in the racing game are usually a very rare thing – and particularly so when they come from someone who is a former employer, close rival and sometime nemesis – but Edward O'Grady insists on describing Mouse's record at Cheltenham as 'wonderful'. This from a man who has trained eighteen Cheltenham winners and is the third most successful Irish trainer at the Festival, after such legends as Vincent O'Brien and Paddy Dreaper.

It should also be noted that this show of respect comes in spite of the fact that the two have not always had an easy relationship, going right back to the days in the early seventies when Willie O'Grady's illness meant that the running of the Ballynonty yard was often left in the hands of Mouse and then head lad, Tim Finn. As Mouse himself says:

> Willie had a lot of good horses back then and it was a great yard to be associated with but when he died in 1972, Edward gave up college [he was training to be a vet] and came back to run the place. Myself and Tim Finn had effectively run the place for quite a while when Willie was sick and it was initially probably a little difficult for Edward when he had to come home, because the owners used to ring us up instead of him and that probably led to an amount of fractiousness, but we got on with it.

Timmy Hyde, who was the professional for many years with Willie O'Grady, remembers this time and he is firmly of the belief that much of the education Mouse got for his future career as a trainer was at the Ballynonty yard: 'Mouse and Tim Finn, the head lad, would have had a lot to do with the training there when Willie was not in the best of health. They had a lot more to do with it than if Willie had been in better health, so there was a good learning period there for him.'

Tom Busteed, who would become the stable amateur at Ballynonty before going on to become a legend in his own right as a horse-breaker, confirms as much: 'It was before my time there, but I know that when Willie O'Grady was ill, Mouse and Tim Finn basically ran the show. Tim would have been able to sort out the daily routines for the horses and between the two of them they would make the entries. For Mouse, that was an invaluable grounding which would pay off later.'

It would be churlish to say other than that Mouse and Edward O'Grady enjoyed a healthy, if unspoken, disregard for each other – then and now – and Tom Busteed probably sums up best how that situation came about:

> There was always a bit of antipathy between Mouse and Edward, because Edward didn't really like the way Mouse did things and vice versa. That materialised more when they parted ways. In the training ranks – amongst most trainers – there is a huge jealousy factor. It goes throughout the whole industry in fact. There is the whole thing about, 'Why did he get that good horse and not me?' or worse, an owner of yours sending horses to me, which happens all the time. Worse again is an owner having a horse with one trainer and taking him away to send to another trainer – that is the complete pits. When that happens you're wishing nothing but bad on the horse – not to mention the guy who now has it.
>
> With Mouse having been the jockey at a major yard, it was only natural that he'd take business away from there when he went training. From my point of view, I've always had the highest respect for Edward because he's such a shrewd guy; he's so dedicated and has such a good, mature team there. But there is no question about it; there was antipathy between them. It was not so evident when Mouse was riding for Edward, but much more apparent when he left. That would have been a natural course of events within the game.

O'Grady himself does not – understandably – fully agree: 'I think there is room for all of us in this game and finding rich punters was obviously a long suit of his. Initially I know where he got his first owners from: he got them from me. But there is no doubt that his father and his father's presence in racing was a great asset to him and I'm sure he used that to good effect; it certainly didn't do him any harm.'

Mattie Ryan reckons it is very uncommon for a top jockey to become a top trainer but he maintains that Mouse's attention to detail right from the start always set him aside: 'His horses were always turned out properly and back in the days when they first started giving out prizes for the best turned-out horses at the races, Mouse used to win them all because his horses were always beautifully presented.'

As far as finishing his life as a jockey and going into training, Mouse is, as ever, succinct:

> I started training in 1979 and I had my first winner in 1980. I was actually still riding at that point, but it was after catching up with me. I was in a fairly wicked physical state. Over the years I'd broken my ankle, my tib and fib, my knee, my arm, a couple of fingers, a couple of collar bones, a couple of vertebrae, a hip, a couple of noses and, of course, concussions to beat the band. Back in those days though, concussion wasn't a big deal and you could ride away even if you were half-zonked.

Whatever he might have thought about his chances of success in the training ranks, there were plenty of others willing to throw cold water on his aspirations and there were considerable doubts among some racing's insiders that Mouse would make the grade as a trainer. Tom Busteed puts people's misgivings into context:

> It was definitely a surprise to me at the start that Mouse turned out to be such a good trainer. He was never really hands-on in O'Grady's. He'd come in on a Wednesday morning and a Saturday morning to do work. He'd do that and he'd be gone. He was not involved with the horses in terms of breaking them or anything. All he had to go on was from what he saw and what he felt himself. But whatever he got from that, he definitely took it all in and put it to good use when he put his own ideas to it.

While one thought that Mouse was just doing his job riding, he was actually doing an awful lot more than me or anyone would have reckoned. I was amazed and astounded at how good he became. The way I would describe it is that what he took out of Edward's was more what he was *not* going to do rather than what he *was* going to do. Mainly that consisted of not trying to extract the most out of horses when they were early in their careers. Having worked with both of them, I think Mouse decided that, having seen the training regime of the young horses at O'Grady's, he decided not to go down that road.

Look at someone like Fred Winter. He was inclined to tell an owner of a five-year-old to take it away for a year because it wasn't ready. In England then you had owners who would wait and you'd see Winter producing horses at six years of age and that's why so many of his went on to win Gold Cups: they were preserved. The fella who has a plan and who puts them away for a year after they win their point-to-point and then runs them in a couple of hurdles is beginning to develop a chaser. They have to be developed: they need time these horses.

Ted Walsh reckons that Mouse's early problems with the educational system actually taught him a lot:

He had problems which they didn't realise and in those days you got a rap around the head and were told you were a stupid fucker. But he got over all that and he's proved the system was wrong. I mean look at just how few people have trained a Gold Cup winner, for example. The likes of Edward O'Grady, who is hugely successful, has never won one; Nicky Henderson never even had a runner until both Marlborough and Bacchanal ran the first year Best Mate won it – not even a runner, not to mind a winner – and he's one of the most prominent trainers in the UK. Martin Pipe never won a Gold Cup and he was Champion Trainer a heap of times. Six or seven of the top trainers in Ireland in recent years – Noel Meade, Willie Mullins, guys like that – have never won it. Mouse has won though and it doesn't matter if he never wins another one because his name is already on the board. All he can do now is go and win it again.

As a trainer I've always had the greatest respect for him and when I rode for him I think there was a mutual respect between the two of us because we knew each other for so long.

Another man who was not at all surprised that Mouse went on to become a successful trainer was Brian Lusk, the man who trained Skymas, giving Mouse his two Champion Chase victories back in the 1970s: 'He was always mad about horses and his whole life revolved around them, so that wasn't a surprise. He might not have had a horsey background, as such, but he knew as much, if not more, than many who had.'

For all that though, Lusk feels that there were times in his training career that Mouse was somewhat lackadaisical:

> I think sometimes he was just a bit too laid-back though and, while he has been very successful as a trainer, I think he could have been even more successful. He was too fond of hunting. Things like the bailiff arriving, or the taxman coming after him should never have happened. He is well liked, no doubt, but he was his own worst enemy, in my book.

Lusk is alluding to some of the darkest days in Mouse's career as a trainer. Mouse himself will readily confess that he is undoubtedly a terrible businessman and one for whom the day-to-day running of the business affairs at Everardsgrange was initially a nightmare: 'Going training was probably the last thing I wanted to do. I was flat broke and could hardly afford cigarettes for the week. The situation was not bad – it was diabolical. I'd never heard of cash flow, not to mention a business plan. If I wrote a cheque it was touch-and-go as to whether the bank manager would honour it.'

However, he defends his hunting interests vehemently as he says that had he not been involved, he would not have met many of those people who would later play such a big part in his career – Mrs Valentine, Demi O'Byrne and Timmy Hyde, to name but a few.

★

Finding a base from which to work was an initial concern. Returning from hunting one day, he passed a smallholding just outside Fethard. At that stage he had already developed one farm at Ballykelly, but this new place – Everardsgrange – was a place he really felt could do the trick. Demi O'Byrne was later to buy Ballykelly from Mouse, as he relates:

> The first farm Mouse bought was at a place called Ballykelly, over near Cashel, and that was total virgin country altogether – there was nothing there but bushes and ditches and fields. He developed the whole place and he turned it into the most magnificent model farm you could want. He laid it all out with posts and rails and built a lovely yard. Mattie Tynan, who's since done lots of work building yards all over the place, including Coolmore, built it for him. Those were the first stables Mouse ever had and his style and class shone out there. He was breaking horses there and he had a few pointers and so forth, but it was very much a going concern.
>
> After that he bought Everardsgrange and I was living in an old rectory over near Clonmel, but I sold that and I bought Ballykelly from Mouse. It turned out to be a very lucky place for me. There were twenty-five boxes there and there was a small indoor ring as well where we could loose-jump the horses. Some great horses came out of it.

Mouse himself remembers the finding of Everardsgrange as a stroke of luck:

> I found this place after I drove past it one day. I'd been out hunting not long after Shanny and myself got married and we were looking for a place. It was very run down. It was just a house on a half-acre, but it had potential. We originally only bought it to do it up and flog it on, but it didn't work out that way. We bought it off an American who'd bought it to do it up as a holiday home. There was no 'For Sale' sign on it or anything, so we had to do a bit of investigating.
>
> We discovered there used to be a stallion standing here called Major Owen, who was a hell of a stallion, and I think he covered the mares in the next room [pointing to what is now the dining room in his home]. The place was originally owned by a character from Fethard called Dick Gough who had been renting the place

and it was wicked run-down, but the horsey connection was there, even if it was only coincidental.

His ex-wife, Shanny, remembers a very dilapidated premises when she was first taken to see it:

> I remember him coming back and telling me about this place and we went over and had a look. We both had the same feeling that it had potential, even though it was completely run-down. We were going to call it *Neantóg* – the Irish word for nettles – because it was completely covered in them. There was also the carcass of some beast in the room that subsequently became the dining-room. It was a mess.
>
> An American had bought it but all he had done was make sure the gutters were working and he also put a few windows in. That was it. There was a lot of work to be done and we spent a lot of energy and money on the place. We did as much of the work as we could ourselves. The pair of us stripped off the plaster on the outside and repointed all the stonework. Over time we totally rebuilt the place.
>
> There was a horsey connection there because it had been the home of a well-known sire, but I was more interested in renovating the house and creating a garden and things. The horsey end of it was all Mouse's doing. The stone stables were there when we bought the place and we converted them first and then build the wooden ones. Everything else then happened bit by bit.

Mouse now thinks that his transformation from jockey to trainer was a little bit more destined than intended:

> I was looking after sick horses for a while and then someone asked me to train a horse. We only had six boxes when we started. Major Redmond Cunningham from Waterford was my first owner. He'd been a client of O'Grady's and I'd ridden a few winners there for him. Then Nicky Shee, a solicitor from Clonmel, got together with Demi O'Byrne and they sent me a horse called Faugheen. It sort of grew from there.

O'Byrne himself maintains he is still terribly proud of the fact that Faugheen turned out to be Mouse's first winner at Limerick on St Stephen's Day 1980:

> When he started training it was only a natural progression that I would send him a horse. During that time we were very close friends and we did an awful lot of hunting together. Sadly these days we don't see each other very often because I am away so often. But my recollection of Mouse in those days is that anything he did, he did it better than anyone else. He was the first to find Mattie Tynan and invent him as a builder and Ballykelly is still there to this day and is still a model farm. He did the same then when he developed Everardsgrange.
>
> Faugheen was his first winner and I'm glad I had the honour of giving Mouse his first-ever success as a trainer. There was never a question of not giving him a horse. Nicky and I had a few bits and pieces of horses in partnership and that horse ran in Nicky's wife's name. It was a real good performance as he won first time out and it looked like he could be something decent, but then he started bursting blood vessels. It was a short-lived glory. Having won his first outing, he also showed very well next time out, but he bled and that was the end of that.
>
> But there was never anything primitive about Mouse in anything he did. When he went hunting he dressed properly, mounted properly and he'd go like smoke. And when he went about buying a horse, he'd be the same. He is a very good natural judge, particularly for a man with his background. He is quite extraordinary; he is a complete natural when it comes to judging a horse. It may be that such a talent is instinctive in some people, but that's the way he is.
>
> There was never anything primitive about Everardsgrange either, because that is not his style. He might even have been inclined to put the cart before the horse a bit. He might have had nothing himself, but the horses would be one hundred per cent looked after. You might not know where he got the money for the horses but he had them. We went to a lot of sales in those days and he used to come over here to me a fair bit, but he was always able to pick out the best ones – whether he could afford them or not.

Hollywood director and friend of Lord Killanin, John Ford in Connemara surrounded by children, including the Morrises. Eldest, Redmond, sits at far left; John is holding the director's hand; Deborah stands in front of Ford, with Mouse beside her to the right. Sinéad Cusack (now one of Ireland's best-known actresses) is to the right of Mouse. (*Morris family collection*)

Class picture of the boys from St. Conleths, Dublin *c.* 1962. Mouse is on the far left, second row, with his twin John beside him. Fourth from left, front row, is Stuart Kenny, who turned the Paddy Power operation into one of the biggest bookmaking firms in these islands. Third from right, third row, is specialist racing photographer Peter Mooney. *(Peter Mooney)*

Mouse's father – also Michael Morris, but better known as Lord Killanin – is pictured here in thoughtful mode. (*John Morris*)

Mouse aboard Edward O'Grady's Kilmacillogue at Leopardstown, clearly illustrating his neat and tidy technique as a jockey. (*Mouse Morris*)

Mouse seen here on Edward O'Grady's beautiful grey Prolan in the 1976 Aintree Grand National. (*Mouse Morris*)

'Going like smoke . . .' Mouse, trademark cigarette in his mouth, out hunting on his beloved Jerome. (*Mouse Morris*)

All dressed up for the hunt: Mouse with sons Christopher (right) and Jamie getting ready for a day's hunting. *(Mouse Morris)*

Then stable jockey Tommy Carmody reckoned that Buck House (nearest camera) was 'as good a jumper as I've ever ridden'. Seen here at Punchestown in 1985, demonstrating the fluid style which saw him win a Queen Mother Champion Chase the following year. *(Healy Racing)*

An aerial view of Everardsgrange, near Fethard, Co. Tipperary. In the centre is the main house, surrounded by the original boxes which were there when Mouse bought the premises. The remaining boxes back onto the all-weather gallop, at left. *(Mouse Morris)*

A smiling Tony Mullins (on left) and a pensive-looking Tommy Carmody with their respective partners, Dawn Run and Buck House, ahead of the unique Match Race between the two at Punchestown in 1986. *(Healy Racing)*

The tough-as-nails Attitude Adjuster – named by his owners after a potent cocktail – would become Mouse's second Cheltenham winner with the equally tough Ted Walsh aboard. *(Healy Racing)*

Mouse discusses the outcome of a race with multiple champion jockey Tony McCoy. *(Healy Racing)*

This cartoon was contributed by a sixteen-year-old girl from Cork after Ted Walsh said that he showed Attitude Adjuster the video of his victory at Thurles prior to his Cheltenham win. *(Irish Field)*

An inauspicious start: War Of Attrition crumples on landing while leading a point-to-point at Horse And Jockey in March 2003 by twenty lengths. *(Healy Racing)*

Mouse and jockey Conor O'Dwyer ponder tactics in the parade ring before War Of Attrition's chasing debut at Thurles in November 2004. Their concerns were unfounded as the horse won comfortably. *(Healy Racing)*

Mouse and Michael O'Leary mull over War Of Attrition's second place in the Lexus Chase on unsuitable ground at Leopardstown in December 2005. *(Healy Racing)*

Conor O'Dwyer pilots War Of Attrition around the outside in the Cheltenham Gold Cup in 2006. *(Peter Mooney)*

Winning connections: Mouse with Anita and Michael O'Leary and Conor O'Dwyer celebrate War Of Attrition's Gold Cup win amid joyous scenes in the winners' enclosure at Cheltenham. *(Peter Mooney)*

Exultation: Mouse and Conor O'Dwyer in an emotional embrace after War Of Attrition's Gold Cup win in 2006. *(Peter Mooney)*

The winning team with the spoils of War: (from left) Mouse and EJ the dog, with staff Johnny Cummins, Oonagh Barrett, War Of Attrition, Noelle O'Gorman and Tom Crotty. *(Healy Racing)*

Taking the rough with the smooth: Mouse discusses what happened to Skibb with jockey Andrew Leigh after the jockey pulled the horse up at Cork in April 2007. *(Healy Racing)*

Paddy Flood is one of Ireland's top up-and-coming riders and one who Mouse rates very highly, which is probably why he hired him as stable jockey in 2007. The duo hit the jackpot with Hear The Echo in the Irish Grand National at Fairyhouse in March 2008. *(Healy Racing)*

The grass gallops at Everardsgrange are regarded by many – including former stable jockey Conor O'Dwyer – as being among the finest in these islands. *(Mouse Morris)*

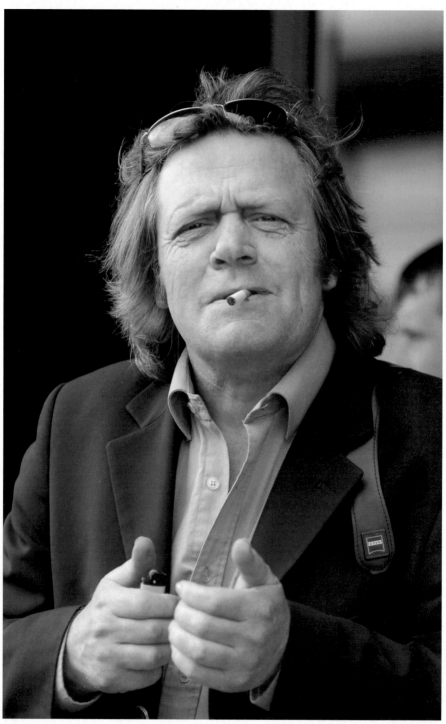
Fuelling the habit: Mouse lights a trademark cigarette outside the weighroom at Punchestown. *(Healy Racing)*

Venalmar on his way to second place in the Ballymore Properties Novices' Hurdle at Cheltenham in March 2008, ridden by Paddy Flood. *(Peter Mooney)*

Skating home: Hear The Echo was a surprise 33/1 winner of the Irish Grand National at Fairyhouse in March 2008 when ridden by Paddy Flood. *(Peter Mooney)*

With a mischievous look in his eye, Mouse is caught by photographer Pat Healy with the ever-present cigarette in hand. *(Healy Racing)*

That's how he got on so well in the long run. Since he started out training, he never needed anyone to tell him anything about horses.

This is a theme picked up by Conor O'Dwyer, a man who would have huge success with Mouse as the stable jockey at Everardsgrange. Conor maintains:

> The horses are really a passion with him and he takes everything in when he's around them. That has obviously stood to him. Riding for him I always got on great, because he is brilliant in the fact that the first thing he ever said to me was that all he wanted to know was the truth. A lot of trainers will persevere with bad horses, but not Mouse. If it was not good enough, he didn't want to feed it in the morning – he wanted to get rid of it. A lot of trainers, from a business point of view, would want to keep the horse and give it every chance. But not Mouse: there was never any grey area with him – the horse was either in or out. For a jockey that's brilliant, because you're not coming in after a race trying to think of things to say. If you genuinely feel the horse is no good, you just say it. That takes pressure off you.

His point about the business end of things is very prescient, since this was something that was to dog Mouse throughout his early training career, as Shanny explains:

> It was quite hand-to-mouth at that stage and the one thing we hadn't really a clue about was how much money would have to go into the place to create a training establishment. I suppose we were consumed by youthful enthusiasm and, in many ways, money was incidental and that got us into rather a lot of trouble. Maybe it was that the banks were a little bit too generous in those days. We just wrote the cheques and kept going. We put the circular gallop in next door and away we went.

Demi O'Byrne has, perhaps, a more objective view of the situation, maintaining that Mouse always aimed to be an old-fashioned, proper trainer, with a small number of good horses who are looked after in the most impeccable way:

That is not always achievable, because it is costly to try and make ends meet training a small string. The more simplistic way to go about it is to have two hundred horses and hope that you've a Gold Cup winner amongst them. He's stubborn and he's not for changing – and why should he with his record?

I'm not involved in jumpers really anymore, but if someone were to ask me for my advice, I'd say you could not find anyone better in the British Isles to trust to spend your money. He's a very, very good judge: he'll do the right thing and if he comes across a good horse, he'll achieve everything. And you'll have the added bonus that the horse will see out a long career.

It is no good getting a beautiful horse and having him win his Bumper first time out and then he's history. Not that I'm critical of that happening either, but that has been Mouse's way and that's the way he sets out about these things.

As an owner you get the truth about your horse and, in a lot of cases, it might even be an overdose of the truth. The modern trainer often trains as many as two hundred horses and there are not too many wealthy gentleman-trainers out there anymore. Most places these days are huge commercial operations, with big staffs and big overheads. But Mouse has never gone down that road and nor does he want to; he has followed his own path with the full knowledge that the consequences for him financially might not be great.

★

Everardsgrange developed into a fine training establishment over time and also into a family home for Mouse and Shanny. Times might have been tough financially, but they were happy times too, remembered with great fondness by the now long-separated couple.

Their two boys were born into the household and Shanny remembers that, after Jamie was born in 1983 and Christopher came along in 1985, bringing them up in Everardsgrange was a delight: 'Bringing up kids is always a thrill and Everardsgrange was a good place to bring them up because there was so much activity around the place and they had so many friends nearby. The children made our marriage. When they came along they made our lives.'

Those words might ring cold in the light of the subsequent painful and protracted separation the couple went through, but they are voiced with feeling, as is her assertion that 'Mouse is a good dad and he loves his kids and they love him'.

For all the happiness within the family at the time, the persistent financial worries were not going away and Shanny remembers only too well the occasions when those problems festered:

It was a very frightening time when there were bailiffs calling to the door. I think the most frightening thing was that they had the most unbelievably bad manners and asked me to leave the room when they were going through my house. Then to discover they had parcelled things up and removed them was awful. It was the most horrible situation ever.

It was a combination of a lot of things: renovating the house, building everything that was required for the horses – the gallops and so forth. We just wrote the cheques and never really looked at the bottom line. Things went haywire there. There was an accountant who was supposed to be advising us, but we did not get good advice from him – that's for sure. The fact that we were raising a young family at the time only made it even more terrifying.

We were both extremely lucky that we had families that pulled in behind us. Both my parents and Mouse's parents were good to us. We were very lucky and not many people are that fortunate. I don't know where we would have been without that. Even outside our families, there was a huge amount of goodwill among the owners and friends for us. Again, we were so lucky we had so many loyal friends who were willing to help. Michael Purcell and John Magnier were particularly good.

Demi O'Byrne's assessment that Mouse is a trainer and not a businessman is very accurate. He is not in any way commercially driven; it is all about the horses.

I remember at one point, when we only had about twenty horses, being advised that we needed forty to make it pay.

But, even in lean times, Mouse was always able to find new owners. Things might have been particularly lean in terms of the bank account, but he always succeeded in getting new owners and new horses. He was always able to find them and he has always been very direct with owners about the ability of their horses.

He never really wanted a yard with a hundred and fifty horses in it. Certainly there are very successful trainers who have those numbers, but it must be very, very difficult for them every day to monitor them properly and to assess their ability. It has to be easier when you've fewer horses. That was always the way he wanted to operate. He always wanted to give his horses personal attention, rather than relying on an assistant, or whatever, to help him out. He was always very hands-on with the horses. As I am not horsey at all, I probably took for granted how intuitive he is with horses. I would have assumed that without realising it.

Alfie Buller, now the master of Scarvagh House Stud in Northern Ireland and a property developer, reckons that Mouse was not having the best of runs at that period of time and had 'a few' financial problems:

Those were rough times for the kid and I gave him advice about dealing with the bank. I had a boat down on the Med and we used to go on holiday together. Shanny and the boys came too and it was good craic, although I remember he wouldn't eat the food on the boat and all he would eat was ham sandwiches. He is an eccentric and very wonderful fellow.

While we kept in touch, we saw less and less of each other. We had a few other horses with him after Mixed Blends, but there were no superstars. We've always had bits and pieces with him.

Mouse himself says that it was owner Vincent Daly who was the biggest help to him in terms of sorting out his financial problems: 'Vincent was magnificent and he was like a father to me in many ways. If it had not been for him I don't know what might have happened.'

In those early days, however, even his best friends doubted him sometimes and Demi O'Byrne recalls, with considerable regret in his tone, that there was one occasion when those doubts led to a bad misjudgement on his part: 'We had a horse with him – John Magnier, Timmy Hyde and myself – and Mouse said he was a good horse, but we didn't believe him and we insisted that we sell it on. It later transpired he was a good horse and he won a lot of things in England.'

Alfie Buller remembers the incident, remarking, 'I think one of the hardest times I felt for him was when he had a horse called You're

Welcome which was sold to Charlie Mann and which then went and won loads of times. Every time the frigging horse won, I felt sorry for Mouse.'

★

If other people were feeling sorry for the trainer, he was most certainly not feeling sorry for himself. He took the good with the bad and accepted the vicissitudes of the constantly turning wheel of life. He got on with developing Everardsgrange as best he could – or as best as his financial situation would allow. His uncanny knack for relationships with friends and owners (often one and the same folk) kept the show afloat. Amongst those who kept the faith and the yard in horses, Mouse numbered people such as John Magnier, Demi O'Byrne, Tony O'Reilly (later to become Sir Anthony O'Reilly), Alfie Buller, Michael O'Flynn and many others, including Eddie Jordan (after whom Mouse's current dog, EJ, is named) and Michael O'Leary at a later date.

There were other supporters, too, and one of the best was close neighbour, Mrs Bridget Selby-Biggs, who owned the nearby Brook Hill estate. Shanny remembers a very kindly, elderly woman who was quite smitten by her new, youthful neighbours:

> We were very lucky because Bridget lived across the road and she was a wonderful woman who was only too delighted to let us use her land, which Mouse eventually bought and that is where the grass gallops now are. She was a real character – long dead now, sadly. She loved horses and had originally come over from England to hunt and had bought Brook Hill because she liked the idea of living here. She was quite invalided when we knew her, but she just loved the idea of having horses in her yard and all the activity that went with it.

Those grass gallops proved to be a real bonus, as it transpired and Conor O'Dwyer reckons they are one of the most valuable assets at Everardsgrange:

> They have always stood to him and, in my opinion, they are among the best in the country and they have definitely been a contributory

factor in the development of all the good horses he's had there over the years. It may have been that Paddy Mullins trained a Gold Cup winner in what, effectively, was his back garden, but you have to cope with whatever you are used to and in Mouse's case he is used to having those excellent facilities.

Up to his neck in debt – but reasonably happy for all that – Mouse was on the road as a trainer with a nascent establishment and a few horses. Now all he had to do was find a few winners. No one could have realised then that he would clock up that 'wonderful' Cheltenham record so graciously described by Edward O'Grady.

7 Buck House

'He won the Supreme Novices' Hurdle in 1983, finished fourth in the Champion Hurdle in 1984 and second in the Arkle in 1985. Then he won the Champion Chase in 1986 and then he died.'

Mouse's matter-of-fact summation of the career of the horse that put him on the map as a horse trainer is typically succinct but does no real justice to an animal that was one of racing's superstars in his era. While he might not have been in the class of an Arkle or a Best Mate, he was nevertheless a sensation in his prime and, had it not been for the appearance at the same time of a mare called Dawn Run, it might have been him – rather than her – who is enshrined in the collective memory of the racing community.

★

Mouse bought Buck House at Goffs in 1981 for 12,000 guineas which, he admits, was a sizeable enough chunk of money back then:

> He was by Royal Buck out of Slave Dee and was owned by Bobby Lanigan who later became an integral part of the Coolmore operation. I think he was bred in Doran's down in Wexford – Caher-villahow would later come from the same place. He was three when I bought him and he was for Michael Purcell – the cattle dealer – who was a great friend of mine. He told me he wanted the horse for his brother, Seamus, because he was working flat-out and needed something to take his mind off work. Being a typical trainer I said: 'Jaysus, I have one – and he'll win next week.

Purcell's fellow cattle dealer, John Horgan from Cork, recalls the moment Buck House was sold by Mouse to the Purcells:

> We were in the Horse and Jockey [a famous watering hole on the main Dublin–Cork road] one day – myself, Michael Purcell and Mouse – and he [Mouse] was telling us he had a good horse. I remember saying that I had enough horses at the time, but Michael said his brother Seamus had no horse and he'd buy it for him. It turned out to be a good deal.

Despite the trainer's initial optimism, the horse didn't win in the week following his sale, or any week soon after that in fact. Instead he recorded a string of disappointing second places, which was exceptionally frustrating for the nascent trainer and the connections. 'He was coming home on his own one day in a Bumper at Listowel when he jumped out over the fucking rails about a furlong from home,' Mouse remembers incredulously. 'He just took flight. I don't know what startled him.'

Head lad Liam Burke says that on that day in Listowel he thought Buck House was the 'greatest certainty that ever went to the races'. As the race progressed, the horse did indeed look certain to win, leading as he was by some ten lengths, and Burke says that as he turned into the straight, he must have felt that jockey John Queally was going to hit him and 'he just leapt the rail and jumped out onto the chase course.'

Tommy Carmody, stable jockey from 1983, recalls the Listowel incident and reflects that, luckily, nothing like that ever happened to him when he took over the ride on Buck House: 'Thank God he was never like that with me and I have to say that, by the time I got to ride him, the stand-out thing about him was his jumping. He was fast and accurate, be it either hurdles or fences. He wasn't an over-big horse but he was as good a jumper as I've ever ridden.'

But there is much more to the story than just those bald facts and the trainer himself obviously has fond memories of the horse which effectively put him on the map: 'I had him from 1981 and he went on to go to Cheltenham for four consecutive years from 1983 to 1986, and he had two wins and a second from those outings, which isn't a bad strike rate. I suppose I thought he was good when he won his first Maiden Hurdle, but he just got better and better.'

Mouse denies that having a star of Buck House's class so early in his training career was the making of him, because the nature of the business is so up and down anyway, but he does concede that having such a good horse and doing so well with him helped put the yard on the map: 'I have been lucky to have had some good steeds, especially for such a small yard, and I've been lucky that pretty much anything I've ran at Cheltenham over the years has been in the money. We have had a few gluggers, of course, but that's only par for the course.'

Liam Burke remembers Buck House being broken when he arrived at Everardsgrange in 1981 and he says he was initially unimpressed:

> I remember riding out one day and one of the lads was breaking him and the horse whipped around on the road. The young fella had the ropes loose and he got his leg caught in them and the horse dragged him down the road a bit. Someone stopped him and he didn't go too far. I won't name the person in question, but I remember he brought the horse into where we lunged them and he nearly killed him. I'll never forget it. He blamed the horse when it was his own stupid fault. Buck House was always a nervous horse, but that was no help – what that fella did to him.

Former Everardsgrange head lad and jockey, Bob Townend, describes Buck House as having been the 'best-fed horse in Ireland'. Every day the gelding got two bottles of Guinness, half-a-dozen eggs, honey and a load of vitamins thrown in with his night feed. 'He was better fed than Arkle,' he laughs.

For all the good feed, Buck House never really shone at home and Townend reckoned 'he wouldn't beat a donkey in a gallop'. Burke, too, remembers a horse who was 'never flashy at home' but who, when he eventually went jumping, was 'a pure athlete'.

The trainer himself recalls a horse that was initially 'a bit kinky' and did not like anyone approaching him from his right-hand side. That did not explain the wild manoeuvre at Listowel where he frightened the gizzard out of the unfortunate Queally, but Mouse reckons they were able to straighten him out with the use of an American-style run-out bit. After this was adopted the horse hardly ran a bad race.

Mouse says that the first year Buck House was sent to Cheltenham to run in the two-mile novice hurdle, then called the Waterford Crystal

Supreme Novices' Hurdle, he was the least fancied of the Irish runners on the day and was sent off at the decent price of 8/1. 'Whatever about the rest of them, we certainly fancied our fella that day and the Purcells had backed him.' They weren't the only ones and the win was one which was feted in many quarters as a touch rightly landed.

Tommy Carmody, stable jockey from 1983, reckons that Mouse actually did a 'fantastic job' to iron out the horse's all-too-obvious problems: 'Having the kink that he had and yet turning out to be the horse he eventually became was a big turnaround, and Mouse deserves the credit for that. If he had been handled wrong, he might have gone the opposite way and become impossible, but Mouse got it right with him. It wasn't luck.'

Carmody recalls that in the run-up to Buck House's bid for the Supreme Novices' title, he actually had the option of riding several other horses in the race, but he was very content to stick with the Everardsgrange entry:

> The manner in which he won his Bumper and the rate of improvement he'd shown as a novice told me all I needed to know about him. It is hard sometimes to tell someone just how good a horse feels when you ride him in work, but throughout that build-up I could tell that this was a really good horse and an improving one too. I knew he was spot on and, as events transpired, I was right.

Liam Burke also felt that the horse was clearly a good thing going to Cheltenham and highlights Mouse's ability at getting a horse ready for a big day: 'He has always been a brilliant man to lay out a horse for Cheltenham. He always had three or four for the Festival and he always had them right for the day. The first time we saw that was with Roadway. There were only one or two good days in a year for that horse, but Mouse kept him for those days.'

Jim Delahunt of the *Sunday Herald* in Scotland would later write: 'Television pictures showed Buck House's paddock sheet being thrown into the air just past the winning post, the unmistakable cartoon drawing of a mouse's face on the brown material drawing the viewing public's attention to the fact that more than a few people had an inkling and that this was a touch well and truly landed.'

That Buck House was considered good enough to go back to Cheltenham the following year and contest the Champion Hurdle was significant and, although he only finished fourth to the horse that would ultimately turn out to be his bête noire, Dawn Run (to whom he would lose on each of the seven occasions he ran against her), the connections even then knew there would be a lot more to come when he faced bigger obstacles. 'He didn't perform too badly in that Champion Hurdle,' Carmody remembers, 'I seem to remember having him upsides with Dawn Run at the second last, but she was a fantastic horse and the best of her sex I've ever seen, so it was no disgrace to lose to her that day.'

However, in spite of the horse's excellent performance over hurdles, Mouse knew that when he took to fences, he could be better still: 'We'd schooled him over fences from the time he was three and we knew that he'd take to them.' This assessment is backed up by Bob Townend, who thinks that it was really only when Buck House was sent chasing that he came into his own:

> He was fierce lazy at home, but even when we schooled him he loved to jump a fence and was very confident right from the off. He'd just see a fence and he'd ping it. He was something else, he'd no fear. If you schooled him with anything else, he'd be in the air when the other horse would be taking another stride. A complete natural.

Liam Burke concurs and says that when the horse first saw fences he was 'like a cat' but the big worry was that he never did a tap at home and never beat another horse in a gallop.

While none of the Everardsgrange team at the time was incorrect in their judgement, Carmody thinks that if he had won the Champion Hurdle in 1984 he would have gone on to win several others, but also reasons that the fact he was beaten only opened other doors:

> We were very excited with him as a chaser right from the off and he won some good races in Ireland throughout the campaign leading up to the Arkle at Cheltenham, so we were very excited about his prospects. In the race itself he travelled and jumped really well until the second last in what was a wickedly fast race, but he

just didn't see it out and he was beaten by Andrew McNamara's Boreen Prince.

So the horse was brought back into the one of the most unwelcome places in the horse-racing world – the second-place position in the Cheltenham winner's enclosure. Nobody knew at the time that there was an explanation for his failure, but his trainer remembers it well:

He burst a blood vessel in the Arkle – something which we didn't discover until the night of the race – so there was a genuine excuse for his defeat at the hands of Boreen Prince. But the thing is that horses often burst once and it never happens again. Nobody really knows why it happens. A lot of people said to me that I'd never get the horse right again after that, but I told them, 'I will, because he's a good horse.' Of course, we were only really hopeful rather than confident.

Mouse got a bad fright, however, just weeks before Cheltenham when Seamus Purcell, having watched the horse race at Ascot, came down from the stand and announced he wanted to leave the horse in England and that Mercy Rimell was to take him over. Mouse says, 'I suggested that was not really a good idea so close to Cheltenham and advised him he could do what he wanted with the horse after the Festival. I don't know what was going through his mind at the time but, in the heel of the hunt, the horse stayed with me.'

The combined hopes and dreams of the connections finally came to fruition twelve months after the disappointment of the Arkle when Buck House won the Champion Chase and gave all concerned their second Cheltenham Festival victory in four years.

After Buck House won the Champion Chase, Mouse got a call from the owner's wife, Philomena, who said she wanted to see him. 'I was expecting to get a wad of notes, but she turned up and gave me a plastic lighter with "Purcell Exports" written on it. It wasn't quite what I had anticipated.'

If Mouse felt he hadn't got his just desserts, there was no complaining among the stable staff. Large amounts of their hard earned had been backed on the horse and the celebrations when he won were long and joyful. 'We all had money on him and I'd say all the customers in McCarthy's were on him as well,' Townend says.

Frank Berry rode in many races against Buck House – on the likes of Antarctic Bay, Lucisis and Bobsline – and says there were quite a lot of good horses around at the time: 'The thing was that Mouse did a marvellous job with Buck House and to be able to bring him back to Cheltenham every year was a feat in itself. He always ran well there and even when he didn't win, he always put up a good display.'

★

Despite such endorsements, many years on it still rankles with connections that when it comes to rating the merits of the various winners over time, their horse is not classed among the top rank. Both Mouse and Carmody maintain these rankings are entirely subjective and depend on the competition in any given year. They also point out that Buck House died a few months after the Champion Chase and never got the chance to defend his crown – a factor that may ultimately have tainted his record. Carmody explains:

I've seen some of those ratings over the years and I have been shocked by what some of them throw up or, more importantly, by the horses that get left out. A horse can only beat what shows up on any given year and it is very difficult to compare one year with another, for a variety of reasons. The bottom line is that the Cheltenham Festival is the crème de la crème of National Hunt racing and he won one of the biggest races at that Festival.

The fact that he won twice at the Festival only adds to that legacy and the fact that he went there four times in total and was only out of the frame once underlines the fact that he was a very special horse indeed and that he deserves to be remembered as being among the best National Hunt horses this country has ever seen. He was a one-off – a great horse.

In recent years when Mouse was raving in the press about how good War Of Attrition was and comparing him with Buck House, I'd ring him and tell him that until he won at Cheltenham he still had a lot to prove. It was only when the horse won the Gold Cup that I rang him to say he was probably right. But the thing is that good ones don't come along very often and you have to know what to do with them when they do. Mouse has always had that ability and he showed that very early in his career when Buck House came along.

Conor O'Dwyer, who is now training in his own right, recognises the potential pitfalls of having such a decent beast in the yard in a nascent career:

> The trouble with having a great horse like Buck House so early is that it can backfire on you because you might believe the game is easy. Mouse is a good example of how difficult the game is, not how easy it is, and he's come through some very tough times and managed to keep the show on the road. Even in very tough times and when he was not getting winners at Cheltenham, he always managed to pull something out that won something decent at Liverpool, or Punchestown, or wherever, even if they were not top-grade horses.

Redmond Morris remembers the family being 'extraordinarily proud' that Mouse achieved so much with Buck House in his early career: 'As a family we were all caught up doing our own thing and so we were not really concentrating on what Mouse was doing at that time, but nothing he did surprised us. We were really pleased, of course, when he won the Champion Chase, but one sort of expected him to do things like that. That was Mouse.'

Shanny maintains that it was a great help to the development of the stables that Buck House came along when he did:

> As well as being a great racehorse, he was also a great character in the yard. He was a real individual and I suppose that's underlined by the fact that he was just so special.
>
> I was completely innocent because I had never really had anything to do with horses ... [Mouse] had been dedicated to them since he was fifteen, or whatever. I was just thrown into it at that stage and I was very naive. While I probably thought at that stage that we were lucky, I didn't realise just how lucky we were with him. There was a lot of hard work went in to Buck House – not to mention a lot of Majors! We had a lot of headaches and a lot of worries. But I suppose nothing changes because that's the training game, isn't it?

To have a win in those days was just mega. You didn't just celebrate on the day – it lasted for ages – and you played the video again and again and again. A win really meant something and a win at Cheltenham was just unbelievable.

Tony Mullins reckons that, without doubt, Buck House's legacy in the racing firmament would have been much greater had Dawn Run not got in the way. 'It was a bit like Mill House and Arkle in many ways,' he says. 'He was so unlucky to run into her. They were the two pre-eminent horses of their era and they were just so far ahead of the rest it was incredible. They were stones ahead of any opposition.'

The two were indeed the outstanding National Hunt horses of their era, a fact underlined in 1986 when their respective successes in the Gold Cup and the Champion Chase at Cheltenham led to a memorable match race between the two at the Punchestown Festival.

8   The Match

The enclosed world of horse-racing is rarely propelled onto the front pages of the mainstream newspapers, but such was the case on 23 April 1986 at Punchestown, when the two greatest Irish chasers of their era, Buck House and Dawn Run, took each other on in a one-on-one winner-takes-all match race. In marketing terms it was a match made in heaven, with the reigning Champion Chase winner competing against the wonder mare who had just won the Gold Cup and was – and still is – the only horse ever to have completed a Gold Cup–Champion Hurdle double.

A massive crowd was very much on the cards: this kind of event was a real curiosity in Ireland, although several similarly high-profile races had taken place on the flat in America over the years, including legendary battles between giants such as Seabiscuit and War Admiral in the 1930s, and Foolish Pleasure and the ill-fated Ruffian in the 1970s.

There was £25,000 on offer for the match – an incredible amount at the time – and £5,000 of that was put up by John Magnier, on the grounds that his Coolmore Stud owned Dawn Run's sire, Deep Run. Seamus Purcell also put up £5,000 and the Irish Horseracing Authority put up the rest.

Ted Walsh, then in the infancy of his career as a racing pundit for RTÉ, says it was one of the great occasions of National Hunt racing in Ireland, remembering:

> It was the first match race I remember in Ireland and it had everything you'd need for such a race. Buck House was after winning the Champion Chase and Dawn Run had just won the Gold Cup, so it had all the right ingredients. There was a huge

crowd at Punchestown that day ... I'm sure it could create the same level of interest in the morning if you did it again. It was like a duel.

Although he did not have a direct interest in the race, Frank Berry also remembers the day clearly:

> The match race was a great spectacle and it was probably the case that jump racing in Ireland needed a bit of a lift at the time. Dawn Run, of course, was a wonderful mare and she'd really caught the imagination of the public. She took a while to get the hang of the jumping, but when she did she showed how classy she was. She drew a crowd everywhere she went and this thing caught people's imagination because they were the two best horses around at the time and both of them were at their peak then. But, from Mouse's point of view, Buck House proved that he was capable of minding a good horse and getting him back to Cheltenham year in, year out. That's always a good sign of a trainer.

The trainer – who still has the contract for the match hanging on the wall of the dining room at Everardsgrange – himself feels that racing in Ireland was in something of a fallow period at the time and the match 'got Irish racing going again'. He also remembers that, such was the interest on the day, public transport in Dublin ground to a halt as taxi and bus drivers pulled in to watch it where they could.

Mouse also reveals that there was something of a major scare in the yard before the race, since Buck House had bruised a tendon and needed day-and-night care from vet, John Halley, to have him race-ready. 'Whatever about the excitement on the day, imagine what would have happened if he didn't turn up. It wasn't bad, but John Halley got him right and he was one hundred per cent to run. I genuinely thought he had a chance because everything was in our favour – distance, weight, everything.'

Tony Mullins, son of legendary trainer, Paddy Mullins, rode Dawn Run that day and he recalls that it was the legendary trainer Vincent O'Brien who played a large part in setting the whole thing up:

> What happened was that there was a good race in Gowran which was put onto the calendar quite late and my father accidentally

missed it, something that happened very rarely. It was a race where both Dawn Run and Buck House could have entered, but it didn't work out. Subsequently I was at the Curragh for the Lincoln meeting and Vincent O'Brien came over to me – I didn't even think he knew me – and asked me if I thought my father would be interested in a match race between Buck House and Dawn Run. I said it to my father and he felt that if the money was right he'd be happy to take on anything. It went from there then.

Mullins maintains that the match only happened because Charmian Hill, Dawn Run's owner, decided that money was 'not of much assistance' to her, and Seamus Purcell, Buck House's owner, was a wealthy cattle baron. Each was as steeped in Irish racing lore as the other and both knew that such a match race was worth more to Irish racing than the money involved in staging it. 'It was lucky they owned the horses, because otherwise such a match might not have been a runner, Mullins comments.

Ted Walsh, outspoken as ever, has a rather different take on it:

> Charmian Hill didn't put up a bob. John Magnier put up money, the Turf Club put up money and the Purcells put up money. She put up nothing and she shouldn't have got a shilling, only that she supplied the mare. She put up nothing and collected the whole lot. I'm sure I said it live on the television on the day that she should have got nothing. I wouldn't have given her the time of day, miserable oul' bitch. Everyone knew that Dawn Run would probably win, but she still put up nothing.
>
> There was nothing really in it for Mouse, but he was a sportsman and he was game. He knew it would be good for the sport and it was a great thing to do, especially in the full knowledge that it was likely his horse would be beat. The Purcells too put their money up like men, even knowing they were likely to lose.

Tony Mullins defends Mrs Hill against the some of the charges that have long been laid against her and her motives for taking on Buck House in a one-on-one challenge: 'My memory of it is simply that she felt she had the best horse and if anything wanted to take her on, that was fine. I don't think she was motivated by meanness or greed. She had got a bit power-drunk with the mare at that point and she felt that as she had the best, anyone who wanted to take her on could pay for the privilege.'

When the match was initially proposed, it was thought that Jonjo O'Neill, who had ridden Dawn Run to some of her greatest successes (not least her recent victory in the Cheltenham Gold Cup) would once more get the leg-up at Punchestown, but unfortunately that was not the case, as O'Neill himself recalls: 'I got a fall at Aintree the weekend beforehand and the match was the following Wednesday and obviously I was in hospital, but Tony got back on the mare. It was a very unusual thing, but it was a great spectacle for Punchestown to have the two pre-eminent horses of the era take each other on.'

In Tommy Carmody's opinion, the opportunity to ride Buck House that day was a fantastic thing, the likes of which he never experienced before or since: 'It was a real one-off, two horses doing battle head-to-head. Sure the trip should have suited Buck House more than Dawn Run, but the whole occasion was just brilliant.'

Tony Mullins, on the other hand, was nervous as a kitten in the run up to the match. He had been controversially jocked-off the mare in favour of Jonjo O'Neill for some of her greatest triumphs and the matter raised a considerable degree of controversy in the racing press at the time. Mullins himself remained phlegmatic throughout the debate and, at the time, kept his thoughts largely to himself on the issue of who should ride the horse. This, in spite of the fact that public feeling had it he was very unfairly treated by Mrs Hill when she insisted that Jonjo pilot Dawn Run in the Gold Cup.

The passage of time has allowed him to be drawn on the matter and he now reveals that the issue of who rode the horse was something that was never spoken about in the Mullins' household:

It was never discussed then and it has never been discussed to this day. It was a thing where you had to bite your lip. The most important thing for me was that I didn't want to see my father losing the horse. We also had to keep the mare winning, because if she wasn't, then she was no use to anyone.

But there was definitely a severe sour taste over the riding arrangements and I don't think Doninga [his father's yard] ever celebrated that Gold Cup victory like a Gold Cup victory should be celebrated. There was never a house party or anything like that. Having said that though, without a doubt it was good for the family business – it was great to win a Gold Cup and be the top yard. Even so, the whole thing about the riding arrangements left it all very sour.

Of the match race itself, he says there were obvious fears in the Dawn Run camp that she might have met her match, even if previous encounters had all gone in her favour:

Dawn Run had beaten Buck House on each of the six occasions they had previously met, but in our camp there was still a big fear of Buck House. Without wanting to be too cocky, we'd always felt that the mare could beat anything, but certainly we knew that if there was any little blip in the race, Buck House was there to beat us. She had annihilated everything she'd ever met, apart from Buck House, and he was there to take it off her if anything went wrong. And that was borne out in the match itself.

He says that riding Dawn Run had never been a worry for him, but now that she had won a Gold Cup and was being labelled the 'Queen of Racing', taking on Buck House at his preferred distance of two miles was a daunting task. He adds:

Everything was regular for Buck House and, while I was not worried about getting back up on the mare in terms of her ability, there was a tremendous amount of pressure because of the whole saga about Jonjo and me in the papers. I'll tell you I can still feel the pressure even now, just thinking about it. This was not like racing at Clonmel where you just went for a drink afterwards. This was something you knew would be talked about in racing for years.

If Stephen Spielberg had come up with an idea for a racing film, then he could not have come up with a better plot for a movie that would get people excited. It might have been an anti-climax if one of them had fallen out the back of track or something but, as it was, the unbelievable dream happened as the two of them fought it out to the line. If you'd planned it for fifty years, it could not have worked out better.

Tommy Carmody puts the occasion right up there amongst his greatest memories during a top-class career:

> For me it would not have been too different from riding at Cheltenham, such was the excitement. OK, there were only two horses running, but the fact of the matter was that it created a savage buzz among the Irish racing public and it really caught the imagination of the public at large here in Ireland as well. It was actually a little surreal and unnatural because the crowd that day at Punchestown were five or six deep on the rails.

Of the match itself, Mullins says there was no idle chitchat between the two jockeys as they raced at full pelt around Punchestown's testing and undulating track:

> By Jaysus there was no talk between us. This was a very serious one. We'd raced at Leopardstown at Christmas and there was only one other horse in that race, a thing called Kilkilowen. We went such a pace that day that I remember as we approached the final open ditch Carmody said to me, 'We're not getting paid enough for this speed'.
>
> At Punchestown we went a phenomenal pace again and I remember saying to myself coming to the third last that if I missed it I was beaten. As it happened, Dawn Run got into the butt of the fence and I had to give her a bit of chest room. I lost about a length and a half and I actually thought I was beaten for a second. I knew I'd get badly chastised if I was beaten, even though the mistake had not been my fault.
>
> By the last, the mare had got it back again and we were level going to the fence but I think I nearly fell off with excitement when I saw the stride and I knew I was right before I took off. When I saw the stride I knew it was over. Before she ever took off I knew she'd win, because Dawn Run was not the best at correcting herself, while Buck House was brilliant at it. But once we met it right, we were home and hosed. There was still nothing between us

as we cleared the last, but once she met it right I knew she would not be beaten. The public might not have known it, but I did.

Tommy Carmody had felt his chance was good before the race and he went into it in a very confident mood:

> I was mad about Buck House and I honestly thought he could beat her and it looked like that for a couple of strides going from the second last to the last, but it was a measure of how great she was that she beat him in the end. The two miles was definitely right up my fella's alley, but she was just too good for him and I don't honestly think we'll see the likes of it again. It was a fantastic day and it was great to be involved in the razzmatazz.

Mullins agrees that it was indeed a fantastic day and he says that the hum from the stand that day as those two champion horses and their jockeys thundered around Punchestown was incredible: 'I've ridden a lot of big races at Punchestown but I've never experienced anything like that day. Coming up the straight, the noise from the stand was such that it felt like a headwind against you.'

Even given all those treasured memories of such a special and unique day, Mullins says that if faced with the same set of circumstances he would be reluctant to put two such top horses against each other in the same way: 'This is just something in my own head, but both horses were dead within two months. Head-to-head races with good horses are not healthy for them. I don't like them and I would not do it again. I loved the day and I loved the way everything worked out, but I'd never do it again, no matter what the prize money was.'

★

In June that year, to the dismay of the public at large and the racing public in particular, Paddy Mullins was told by Charmian Hill that she wanted her horse to try and retain the French Champion Hurdle she had previously won at Auteuil in 1984. Many accused her of being greedy and of unnecessarily jeopardising her horse and these accusations peaked to a roar after the horse's unfortunate death in that fateful race. Mullins comments:

Some people still blame Mrs Hill for sending her horse to France – myself included – but Dawn Run was killed racing, while the Purcells' horse died out in a field. It is ironic that both horses were born within a month of each other, raced together all their lives and died within a month of each other. I believe that had Dawn Run survived she'd have won three Gold Cups and maybe Buck House would have won more Champion Chases, but we will never know.

Ted Walsh is in general agreement:

The strange thing in the long run was that the two of them were dead within a couple of months of the race. Ironically, there was only one other match race I remember, which was in Killarney about twelve months after between a horse of Vivian Kennedy's called Flute Player and The Right Touch, owned by Bill Hennessy, who subsequently owned Sublimity, the 2007 Champion Hurdle winner. It was around the time of the All-Ireland football final and they ran in the colours of the Kerry and Galway county teams and, if I remember correctly, both of them broke down and never ran again.

Buck House died of grass sickness despite the ministrations of veterinarian and equine experts: a specialist was even flown in from Scotland in an attempt to save his life – but nothing could be done and, in very sad circumstances, the first coming of Mouse Morris, trainer, was at an end.

Bob Townend remembers the death of Buck House as 'one of the saddest things I've ever been involved with'. The horse had, as he puts it, 'put Mouse on the map' and had not only given confidence to existing owners to provide money for new young horses, but had also attracted new patrons.

A chapter had been closed. Mouse and his team buried the horse at the top of the Everardsgrange gallops. They then retired to McCarthy's in Fethard for the evening and drowned their sorrows in epic fashion. It was the end of a fantastic period for the trainer and all involved with him. The search now began for the next great one.

9 Cheltenham: The Meaning of Life and a Second Winner

There is no doubt that the annual racing jamboree that is the Cheltenham Festival is Mouse's raison d'être and former head lad Johnny Cummins says that the trainer likes to know by Christmas, in any given season, if there are any potential runners in the yard:

> He never kills horses and many of those appearing first time out would need the run. But if he felt there was a Cheltenham horse there, different things would be done with it. They would be given different routines and a change in scenery in order to keep them fresh. He's a great Cheltenham trainer and always has them ready on the day. Even the bad yokes have surprised me by finishing in the frame there. You'll be wondering to yourself, 'Why the fuck are they going there?' and the next thing they'd be finishing second at 40/1, or whatever.

A former smoker himself, he says that Mouse's prodigious cigarette intake accelerates greatly every year as Cheltenham looms: 'I'd say he be doing a hundred and twenty a day, easy enough, in the build up to the Festival. He'd be smoking from the time he got up at six to whatever time he'd go to bed.'

Mouse himself might maintain that 'a win in Thurles is as good as any' but the glint in his eye betrays his true feelings. Conor O'Dwyer, the stable jockey who would ride War Of Attrition to his own second and Mouse's first Cheltenham Gold Cup in 2006, concurs fully, saying that the whole focus at Everardsgrange revolves around one thing – the Festival meeting:

> As a trainer, his real forte is Cheltenham – even with a bad horse. Every trainer has their own way of doing things, but with Mouse the sole focal point is Cheltenham and everything is geared around that. It may be that his horses going there might not have run for three months, but they will be in tip-top order, which is very hard to do. He is also able to call it from a long way off and he can see in very young horses that they are the type you need to go there. He does have an intuitive feel and in many ways he's a bit like Mick O'Toole in the old days. He had no real horsey background either and yet he did amazing things too.

Timmy Hyde, the Master of Camas Park Stud and a legendary jockey, huntsman, breeder and pin-hooker (a person who buys yearlings with the intention of selling them for profit when mature), has had horses with Mouse Morris since the outset of his training career and he reckons that an ability to think long term has been the secret of the trainer's success:

> If he has a good horse, his mind is always on Cheltenham and always on getting them to peak for the big day. He has always struck me as someone who was a quick learner and that applied both to his career as a jockey and a trainer.
>
> He learned how to ride and how to ride well when he was at Frenchie Nicholson's. He'd had some experience in Dublin before he went there, but he really learned how to ride racehorses when he went there. It was the same when he went to O'Grady's and it was like he just soaked everything in – he must have because he certainly got the knack of training horses and he also has the knack of dealing with people.
>
> I would say that nobody gets more from a good horse than Mouse. I don't know anything about the ins and outs of how he does his business or how he trains the horses or what methods he uses, but what I do know is that he is a horseman through and through and that is something which was obvious from the off. The thing is that you either have it or you don't – and he obviously has.

Hyde rightly points out that the natural cycle of a racing yard shows peaks and troughs following a fairly natural progression – particularly for a small yard like Mouse's – and that War Of Attrition's Gold Cup success signalled an 'up' for Everardsgrange:

> The thing about Mouse is that he has always been as good as any of his peers in this business. I wouldn't single out anyone for comparison, but he's up there with the best of them and always has been. I wouldn't say he's better than any of the championship trainers, but he's certainly as good as them and he can fine-tune a good horse to the perfect pitch for a big race.
>
> He's very straightforward, makes sense and doesn't go around corners. A spade is a spade with Mouse and that's why people like him and that's why owners stay with him, because they're getting the truth. There's no bullshit out of him. He tells you what he thinks and while he's not always right – which of us has a crystal ball, after all? – he tells it as he sees it and if a horse is no good, you'll get told quickly. That's a great asset.

★

The first Everardsgrange-trained horse to appear at the Festival was called Roadway, and he was not only to provide success for the yard, but also for a group of owners who would be hugely instrumental in the development of the trainer and his reputation. Mouse himself counts having had Roadway as a large stroke of luck, primarily as he brought home the bacon in terms of landing something of a gamble:

> He was my first horse at Cheltenham. I had actually ridden him to win at Galway and I then bought him off Con Collins. He had been a flat horse and then I rode him over hurdles at Galway and subsequently Michael Purcell and a few others bought him from me. We set him up for the County Hurdle [at Cheltenham] and we were beaten into third by a head and a short head. We backed him from 40/1 into 16/1, I think, and he was my first fancied runner there.

One of the 'few others' was Corkman John Horgan who, like Purcell, was one of Ireland's so-called 'cattle barons', and made huge amounts of money buying and exporting Irish cattle all over the globe, along with several of his many brothers.

He recalls first coming across Mouse when he was racing at Thurles one day and had a horse that was trained and ridden by Francis Flood. Flood ended up in a photo-finish with Mouse, who was riding for Edward O'Grady on the day: 'Everyone there thought Francis had got up and he was immediately made favourite to get the nod in the photo,' he recalls. 'Mouse was actually 2/1 to get the decision, but Francis came in and told me he hadn't got up, so I backed Mouse to win the photo and I saved my money. That was the first time I met him.'

Horgan was among the earliest owners to patronise Everardsgrange and he recalls a young man who was a 'bit of a bohemian' and whose long, flowing hair was not exactly de rigueur for a horse trainer back then. However himself and Michael Purcell, amongst others, recognised early on that however good Mouse had been as a jockey, he was certainly going to cut the mustard as a trainer. Horgan remembers:

> We backed Roadway to win the County Hurdle at Cheltenham. Charlie McCreevy [later to become the Minister for Finance in Ireland and currently a Commissioner with the EU] was the man putting the money on and we got him at a good price – several good prices, in fact. He came to the last hurdle, with Tommy Carberry up, and he was flying, but he took it out by the roots, nearly stopped, and got beaten by a short head.

They had, however, had the perspicacity to back the horse each way and so their efforts did not go unrewarded.

Liam Burke's memory of that race was that Mouse himself had ridden the horse to a place at Naas beforehand – 'he didn't want to win' – but he was ready for Cheltenham: 'I actually thought they had lost their money, but they had backed him each way and they made a few bob as a result. I'll never forget after that race there was a picture of the horse up on a wall in the house in Everardsgrange with the caption – "Operation successful – but the patient died".'

★

As far as Mouse was concerned – and for all the initial goodwill dispensed to him by the likes of the Horgans, the Purcells, the Magniers,

the O'Byrnes and so on – getting owners into the yard was not easy
and keeping them sweet was even more difficult:

> The thing in those days was that you had to be a salesman. The
> problem was that you were selling something that nobody wanted
> and cost a fucking fortune. As an owner you got no return and lost
> your bollix at the same time. We had to convince people it was
> good fun losing their bollix.
>
> But a lot of the owners were not rich people by any standards.
> One such was Eamonn Cunningham from Kilmoganny who was
> not at all wealthy. But, by God, did he pay his bills on time and he
> was always the first in to look after the lads and to look after me if
> he'd had a winner. He owned a horse called Hi Harry which won
> eight or ten races and he was a super fellow. Guys like him were few
> and far between back then.

Hi Harry brings back fond memories for Bob Townend and he
describes him as a 'right little horse' but one who was difficult enough
to keep sound:

> He had a problem with wind-suck and, as a result, the whole of his
> stable was electrified because he'd wind-suck on anything at all,
> and when that happens their belly fills up with air and it doesn't do
> them any good. Even the stable door was electrified. I often forgot
> that and I'd get a bang off it in the morning. It worked with him
> though and even though he broke down a few times, he always
> came back from it and his speciality was the top of the ground. He
> loved rattling off it and he was great value for Eamonn who got
> mighty sport out of him.

Even if Eamonn Cunningham and Hi Harry did really well with Mouse,
the trainer didn't always find it easy to attract new owners on a regular
basis. As he says:

> I am quite a shy guy and back then I was very shy indeed. People
> think I'm arrogant, but I'm not. I was lucky starting off because I'd
> been a jockey and people knew me and that's how I came across
> people like old Major Cunningham, or a lovely woman called Ellie

Prentice-Porter, an American who had a few horses with me. But it was usually all about meeting people at the races or in the pub and telling them 'You've got to have a horse with me.'

Later on I got owners like Sir Anthony O'Reilly, who was actually a friend of the family but I did not know him. I literally said to him that he had to have a horse with me and luckily he sent me one and has continued to do so. I've had great support from friends like Timmy Hyde, Demi O'Byrne and John Magnier, but there are only so many friends you can tap.

According to Timmy Hyde, who has had horses with Mouse almost from the get-go of his training career, it is testament to the trainer that almost all the owners he started with are still patrons of the yard: 'I think that is because he is just such a genuinely nice guy and there is no bullshit about him. He is a genuine honest-to-God fella and people really like him. He is also a great trainer of a good horse.'

Perhaps it was testament to Mouse's burgeoning reputation that in 1983 Tommy Carmody agreed to become first jockey for the Everards-grange yard. Recently returned from a three-year spell with Michael Dickinson in England and then riding freelance in Ireland, although he spent most of his time working with Noel Meade, Carmody says he was only too glad to take up the offer from Mouse:

I don't know what it was he saw in me that appealed to him, but I'd ridden a few for him and we just sort of clicked. I suppose it was important for him to show to owners that he had a known jockey in the yard and it appealed to me because it was a first jockey's job. Whatever it was, it worked out and we got on really well. He had a lot of good young horses and there was a lot of scope there to win races, good races.

Bob Townend highlights the way in which Mouse was never afraid to try new and radical solutions to getting horses back on the right track:

We had a mare there in the early eighties called Mixed Blends, who was owned by Alfie Buller, one of Mouse's longest-standing owners. She was a very good mare and I looked after her myself, but I remember at one stage she was having terrible problems with stiffness in her hindquarters and we couldn't get to the bottom of it. We heard about this guy – Ryan, I think he was called – who was from Kilkenny, who was an acupuncture specialist, and he came down to us a few times and sorted her out. She went on and finished second at Cheltenham – she was a right good mare. That treatment was something which was never really done with horses and the guy himself didn't really know how it would pan out, but he said he'd give it a shot and it worked out.

Other innovations Mouse came up with was the use of alternative therapies such as reiki as well as things like ice-bath treatments for horses with sore and stiff legs and Townend reckons that, long before such treatments were thought of for top rugby or GAA players to allow swift recovery from match-day exertion, Everardsgrange had its own equine version:

> We had all that going long before it ever became popular in other sports and Mouse was really into discovering alternative treatments for the horses. Another one was scoping horses and long before it became a day-to-day thing in most yards, Mouse had bought an endoscope in America and he would scope the horses himself to make sure they were clear of infection. We mightn't always have known what we were looking at, but we had it anyway. Demi [O'Byrne], who's a vet himself by trade, used to slag us that we didn't know which end of the horse we were looking up. But he was willing to try all that stuff when no one else was doing it and the owners were very supportive and I remember Mrs Fanning [Trapper John's owner] telling him that if he wanted machinery or equipment, she'd pay for it. He just wanted to do the right thing for the horses and the owners were very supportive in that regard.

Tony Mullins comments on Mouse's ability to attract and keep owners in the yard:

> That was not pot luck. That was all about his ability to train winners. Not only that, but he has the reputation of being a good, honest man and there was never a fear of Mouse losing top owners

as a result. It is no coincidence that top owners like the Magniers, the Valentines, Tony O'Reilly and Michael O'Leary all pitched up with him. These are very reputable people and they like dealing with similar sorts. Mouse's integrity has never, ever, ever come into question in any way.

We all have this thing about winning and losing and we all want to win, but most high-profile businessmen just want to deal with honest people and Mouse fits the bill. I could name you a hundred other trainers who have fallen by the wayside over the years because they were ignorant and deceitful. But Mouse has always been straight up and people took him for what he is. It might be that he's a poor businessman, but it is his pure ability as a trainer that has kept him there. He truly loves what he does and it is amazing that after nearly forty years in the game in one form or other, he still has that love for it.

Conor O'Dwyer endorses the sentiment, saying that even though Mouse seems to have been around for a couple of lifetimes, he's still actually not that old and he is still as enthusiastic as ever – particularly when he gets a horse that he thinks will go well at Cheltenham. He says:

If the owner lets Mouse do what he wants with the horses, barring an accident I can guarantee you there is not a better man to have a horse right for Cheltenham. If Mouse sees potential from an early stage, he trains them as a Cheltenham horse, he doesn't train them to win an oul' handicap in Navan or somewhere. He always has a plan and he works around that plan. Once he's allowed do that, he does the business.

Tom Busteed thinks that Mouse got his feel for Cheltenham while in Ballynonty, watching how the horses were trained for the Festival:

Of course he would have had his own ideas when it came to training his own horses, but he definitely got the feel for it at O'Grady's. It is a very hard thing to do, to peak horses for Cheltenham, but Mouse obviously learned the knack of it because he's proved it time and again. He would not be as hard on horses as some trainers – definitely.

I remember riding a horse for Edward first time out at Leopardstown belonging to a Corkman called Bill Hosford, and they backed him from 20/1 to 3/1 and he won. They had a great touch, but the thing was that the horse had been to schooling Bumpers loads of times and he was just so ready. But he had been trained hard for that.

If you gave a horse to Mouse I'd guarantee he'd say, 'I'd prefer not to run your horse in a Bumper; if you really want to do that, fine, but I'd prefer not to.' That's the crux of it, because you've a four- or five-year-old being trained really hard – to its utmost – and the horse might never recover from that. As a result, his horses go that little bit further.

He would prefer to start them in point-to-points because it doesn't take half the training and if the horse is classy enough he'll win when he's three-quarters ready. In a Bumper, that same horse won't win because it's all about galloping, hard galloping. There is no question about it and that's why we see a lot more of Mouse's horses over a period of time than we do from other trainers. We've seen him produce horses that are matured to eight, nine or ten years old. During his learning period, he definitely understood about what not to do, rather more than what to do."

Busteed says that Mouse did things differently to others and he gives a good example why:

The thing about the yards back then was that there was always pressure. For God's sake, I got fired out of one place once for winning! It happened on board a syndicate-owned chaser that was being kept for a day. I can't remember where it was, but I do remember the day because it was pouring, it absolutely milled down – and there were no real instructions, apart from the fact that I was to go out and hack around and not get into trouble. That did not mean a lot to me, to be honest, and once we were racing I realised the horse was jumping like a stag.

As we went past the stands I could see the rest of them falling by the wayside. At the third last I was in second and I jumped it three lengths behind and landed three lengths in front. I just sat there and, by the second last, I was ten lengths clear. He ran out an easy winner but when I arrived into the winners' enclosure the atmosphere was very sombre. I was delighted with myself, but there was no word out of the trainer.

The following Monday the trainer called me and said that he had some bad news for me, that our association would have to be terminated.

They all thought I'd had a touch from the win but, to be honest, I didn't even know how to bet and, in any event, I wouldn't have had the money to do so. I was completely shell-shocked. In the end, it was all sorted out before the end of the day: Mouse actually supported me on that occasion because he knew that the horse had been badly placed.

Frank Berry readily endorses the fact that Mouse is a Cheltenham specialist and he points to the unlucky Mixed Blends in the 1988 Waterford Crystal Supreme Novices' Hurdles as an example:

That was the last year I rode there and Mixed Blends went there quite fancied by Mouse, despite the fact that her form didn't look that hectic. But she ran well above herself on the day and I remember something fell at the second last and Peter Scudamore pulled out to avoid it and carried me really wide and she only lost by a fraction. I don't think she ever ran as well again. That was as close as I got to a Cheltenham winner for him.

Mouse's Cheltenham fixation is also noted by Alfie Buller who would become another stalwart Everardsgrange owner. Buller has a very clear memory of his first introduction to Mouse and of the horse that bred success upon success for him:

I first met Mouse because my father and I used to go hunting for a week down south. We'd bring a load of horses down there and we'd hunt with the Golden Vale, the Tipps, the Limericks and so forth. I met Mouse and Timmy Hyde through this and they were mighty men to go and we had a great craic with them.

At the end of the week – this is probably more than twenty

years ago – we got on really well and I said to them that sometime I'd love a horse for Cheltenham. Mouse [typically] said, 'I have a horse', and the cost was £20,000. The horse was called Pat McGee and when we went to get him vetted, he failed the vet and Mouse says, 'Sure, have him anyway.'

He was my first runner at Cheltenham after Mouse gave him to me and when he ran there he finished third in the four-mile chase. After that, I told him to buy me a horse and he bought Mixed Blends for myself and two or three other guys. The others had no real interest, but one of them was called Adam Scott and twenty or more years later, when he got really interested in horses, he realised exactly who he'd been dealing with, who he'd been in bed with. He has a string of horses with Mouse now – Baily Breeze, Baily Mist and so forth – and they are all out of Mixed Blends. She's still a pet up in Scarvagh and is enjoying herself up there.

Anyway, we paid £35,000 or £50,000 for her, which was a lot of money back then for a mare. Mouse said she'd run well in the two-mile novices' hurdle and she finished second at 33/1, after being beaten by Vagador, who was ridden by one of my best friends at the time, Peter Scudamore. Coming around the home turn, Scu ran very wide and took the mare with him and that cost her at least five lengths and she was narrowly beaten. That was the start of a whole campaign with her as she went novice chasing after that and we knocked loads of craic out of her.

★

But there was one horse that proved to be an excellent example of what Mouse was capable of in terms of the unexpected. That horse was a young hunter chaser called Attitude Adjuster who was regarded by most of his connections as being a fairly ordinary campaigner – Mouse would prove them spectacularly wrong. Liam Burke recalls an incident early in the horse's career at a point-to-point when he showed himself to be a lazy horse:

Mouse, he had three horses in a point-to-point at Lisgoold and John Queally was riding Attitude Adjuster. I was riding a horse called Beguiler and Ray White rode a thing called Pat McGee. I was to make the running and I was John's guardian angel – I was there to make sure he had room when he needed it. Jonjo Walsh had a horse called Deep Incision ridden by Frank Codd and, while Attitude Adjuster was a tough horse, he was a desperate lazy so-and-so. Jim Horgan was supposed to look after the betting that day, but he arrived late and I don't know was there any money on, but the plan came to fruition because Frank Codd fell two out and while I was going the better coming to the last, I took a pull and John won by a couple of lengths. Mouse got a fierce fit of laughing afterwards at the fun of it all.

Having already had two successes at the Festival (thanks to Buck House's exploits – his Queen Mother Champion Chase victory having come just the day before), Attitude Adjuster would give Everardsgrange its next victory when the six-year-old won in the 1986 Foxhunter's. Hard ridden by Ted Walsh, he romped home ahead of Further Thought and Mister Donovan to record the jockey's final win over jumps in an amateur riding career which saw him triumph over 500 races. The horse also became the youngest ever to win the race, an honour that still stands today. It was a victory that the connections did not expect – as might be deduced by his 10/1 starting price – but which was no surprise to the trainer. As Mouse says:

I met John Magnier and Robert Sangster in McCarthy's in Fethard some time before the Festival that year and Robert asked me what the best chance I had at the meeting was. I told him that Attitude Adjuster was my best hope and he just started laughing at me. I said the same to Ted beforehand and I don't think he believed me either.

We ran him at Cheltenham with blinkers for the first time and that was the making of the horse for that race. I had brought him away for a bit of work after Ted had won on him at Thurles in his previous race and we tried the blinkers and he was a different horse – there was a huge improvement. Also, he was unbeaten going there, so my confidence was quite justified, I thought. He might have been hard work to ride, but he was still unbeaten either on the track or in point-to-points. He was only really a moderate horse, but hunter chasing was his forte.

Ted Walsh takes up the story:

> I rode lots of horses for Mouse down the years, but the standout
> was obviously Attitude Adjuster, especially from my point of view,
> because he was my last ride over jumps. I actually rode the horse
> quite a bit. I was coming to the end of my career at the age of
> thirty-six at that stage. I rode him in a point-to-point in
> Patrickswell and then I won another point-to-point at Gowran
> and then I won on him in a Hunter's Chase at Thurles and then
> he went to Cheltenham.

Bob Townend recalls the Thurles victory with a little more veracity
than the jockey: 'Ted gave him the mother and father of a hiding that
day. When he got stuck into one, they knew all about it.'

John Horgan remembers that Attitude Adjuster – famously named
after a demon cocktail and hangover cure invented in the Sandy Lane
Hotel, now owned by John Magnier and J. P. McManus– was owned
in partnership between his then wife, Kate, Diane Nagle, Susan Sangster
and Sue Magnier, who had come together to have a bit of fun with
what would turn out to be a very hard-wearing hunter chaser. They
didn't realise how much fun they *would* have.

Ted was said to be the Lester Piggott of the amateur National Hunt
scene at his peak, because he could go to owners and tell them he was
the man to ride their horse to victory and someone else would get
jocked-off as a result. He was also notoriously liberal with his use of the
whip on recalcitrant animals and after his Cheltenham victory there was
a famous cartoon printed in *The Irish Field* – credited to an unnamed
Cork teenage girl at the time – which highlighted Ted's après-race quip
that he had shown the horse the video of the Thurles race prior to his
Cheltenham victory.

Ted himself confirms that he did not believe Mouse when he said
the horse would win at Cheltenham:

> To be honest I didn't think he would win the Foxhunter's. Mouse
> thought he would, but I didn't. I thought he was too tough a horse
> and they were really beginning to crack down on the use of the
> whip. I'd given him a fair old dressing (!) to win his couple of point-
> to-points and his hunter's chase and I thought there was no way I

could I do that at Cheltenham. But Mouse had a great record there and his horses always were primed to be at their best there. He had him in great order and he also stuck a pair of blinkers on him as well, which he had not done before that. I didn't think he'd win, but he did and won well.

Townend says that in actual fact Ted was in shock after the race because he didn't believe it was the same horse he'd ridden at Thurles: 'That race was only three weeks before Cheltenham and he came back into the winner's enclosure saying: "What did you do to the horse? I could hardly hold him".'

Ted comments, 'I didn't know going out that it was going to be my last ride over jumps, but when he won I was coming back into the winner's enclosure and I thought that this was as good enough a way as any of calling it a day. I'd sort of been thinking of retiring after Punchestown a month later, but it didn't get any better than that, so I made my mind up there and then.'

If it was the end of the day for Walsh as a jump jockey (he would subsequently win lots more Bumpers before finally calling it a day and going on into his highly successful dual career as a trainer and pundit, not to mention fathering Ruby, Jennifer, Ted Jnr and Katie), there was still a long night ahead for the celebrating connections, who flew back to Dublin and, on the way home, stopped off in Morrissey's of Abbeyleix, then owned by the legendary Paddy Mulhall. An old-style establishment that has not seen much of a décor change in decades, Morrissey's is characterised by its pot-bellied stove, wooden floors and the grocery-cum-pub atmosphere which is so sadly rarely found in rural Irish bars these days.

'There's an old delivery boy's bike perched over the door there and we had great fun trying to get Mouse into the wicker basket on the front,' John Horgan remembers of the high jinks that accompanied their celebration of a famous victory. 'I think we even tried to put him into that massive cup you get for winning the Foxhunter's and I'm not sure Paddy Mulhall was very impressed. But we had a great night.'

Others recall an act of great sporting magnanimity in the aftermath of the race, when one of the first people into the winners' enclosure to congratulate the connections was J. P. McManus. The renowned gambler had backed his own horse, Mister Donovan (trained by Edward

O'Grady), to beat Attitude Adjuster on the day, but he could only manage third behind the strongly ridden steed from Everardsgrange. J. P. had not only backed his own horse, but also reputedly laid Attitude Adjuster to lose as well and some speculate that his potential losses on the race topped the £1 million mark. Yet, he still had no difficulty in swallowing his disappointment and was only too delighted to be first up to congratulate his friends and rivals.

The Cheltenham bug that had entered Mouse's soul when he was a lad with Frenchie Nicholson was now well and truly of epidemic proportions and his focus for the rest of his training career would rarely stray elsewhere. Sure, there would be other races to be won and other major obstacles to be overcome in his life, but – apart from his two boys – Cheltenham would remain the single primary focal point of his training life.

10 Trapper John

It is something of a surprise to hear a breeding and pin-hooking legend such as Timmy Hyde admitting that few of the many horses he has sent to Mouse Morris over the years were 'of any great consequence'. They may have been winners on occasion, he maintains, but none were equine superstars.

That said, Hyde *was* the man who sold Mouse a horse called Trapper John, who was to become the trainer's third winner at Cheltenham and his second winner of a championship race. By The Parson, out of a mare called Blueola, Trapper John was actually bred by T. W. Nicholson in Urlingford, County Kilkenny, and bought at the Doncaster Sales before being sold on to Mouse.

'There is no greater satisfaction for me than seeing horses I have sold going on to do well,' Hyde relates. 'I love seeing horses like that do well and to have seen Trapper John go on and win a Grade 1 race at Cheltenham was very satisfying. I would not be in business if I didn't sell winners.'

Recalling those days of the late 1980s and early 1990s, Hyde remembers a particularly fallow period for Irish racing, particularly when it came to winning at Cheltenham:

> At that time there was not much money in Ireland and most horses – the good ones anyway – were exported. Most of my horses back then were sold to export, mostly to England. With Trapper John, Mouse was lucky to find an owner in the late Mrs Jill Fanning who would pay the bills, but that was characteristic of him because from the word go he had good owners who could afford good horses. And most of those owners are still with him.

Bob Townend, recalls a really tough horse, but one for whom they expected a different sort of career:

> We had expected him to develop quickly from a hurdler into a chaser, he just seemed that type. But it didn't work out that way because he never took to fences at all. It was funny, actually, because he schooled good and he never got a fright early on in his life or anything, or so we thought; he seemed to just get it into his head that he didn't like fences. I suppose in more recent times the Bowe family's fantastic horse, Limestone Lad, was something similar – he just never took to the fences.

Townend reckons that the making of the horse was that Mouse discovered the quirk in him quickly enough and was able to redraw the plan for him:

> Once it became clear he was no chaser, we knew the stayer's had to be the target because he was so tough and you just couldn't get to the bottom of him. With other horses, they carry you in a race, but with this fella you'd have to be niggling and driving him on or off the bridle and at the end of the day he'd still be galloping. He wasn't a difficult horse to train, although he was a little moody by times. Even so, he was tough out.

Johnny Cummins, later head lad at Everardsgrange, remembers a special horse, one who held track records at Cheltenham, Newbury and Haydock – all at the same time – and who was to become the youngest horse up until then to win a stayer's hurdle at Prestbury Park:

> Oddly enough – and a bit like Buck House – he ran in a lot of Bumpers and it took him a long time to win his Maiden Hurdle, but when he was second in the Supreme Novices to Martin Pipe's Sayfar's Lad, we knew we had something decent. He also finished second at Aintree that year behind the great Morley Street. We sent him chasing then, but he never took to the fences and poor Charlie Swan [top National Hunt jockey], who was just starting off with Mouse, was afraid of his life on him.

Mouse explains that an incident at Galway was probably the reason for the horse's reluctance to take to fences:

> It was in a novice chase there and another horse cannoned into him at the first fence down the back. He had started as favourite in that race and was well fancied, but that incident frightened the shit out of him and we decided shortly afterwards that we would stick to the hurdles with him. That was the right decision because, while he was not a great jumper of fences, he sure was a super hurdler.

According to Swan himself, Trapper John was actually something of a lazy horse and not the greatest of jumpers and he reckons that while the horse should have gone on to be a classy chaser, his flawed jumping precluded any ideas the connections may have had in that regard. As Swan remembers it, 'He'd no spring in him, no scope. Even at the hurdles he'd barely get off the ground. I remember going down to Mouse's to school him and I took a couple of falls off him. I also fell off him at Gowran [in November 1989] and I remember thinking, 'I'm going to get killed if this continues', so the decision was made to send him back hurdling.'

It proved to be a fruitful decision – Trapper John beat all the English staying hurdlers at Haydock and then some classy opposition, including Cloughtaney and Galmoy at Navan on what Johnny Cummins remembers as 'one of the worst day's racing ever, when he went to the start with a quarter sheet on him, it was so cold.' The following March the horse was sent to Cheltenham to run in the Stayer's Hurdle – then sponsored by Waterford Crystal – and was sent off at 15/2 in a 22-runner field. 'He probably would have been favourite, but there was a huge gamble on Mick O'Toole's Fourth of July, who was backed off the board,' Johnny says.

For Swan there is also fond amusement about the victory: 'Mouse always jokes me that he put me on the map with that victory, but it was an absolutely brilliant thrill and it's something you never forget. And you have to remember that the Irish were after having a very bleak time there as we'd had no winner for the previous two years. In fact, Trapper John was our only winner that year as well, so we got all the plaudits.'

Swan says that when he rode for Mouse at Cheltenham the instructions were always the same – 'don't go down the inside' – because his feeling was that horses who did got knocked around too much. 'He certainly thinks these things through before a race,' Hyde confirms, 'and his experience as a jockey would stand him in good stead in that regard. He always has a plan.'

Swan echoes this:

> He told me to go around the outside and that's what I did and I got a good run throughout. I decided to kick on turning in but he was very idle – so much so I was later done for over-use of the stick trying to get him to the line as quick as I could. I was inexperienced too and I probably got a bit excited, or whatever. But we got home by about a length and a half from Liam Browne's Naevog, who was ridden by Tom Taaffe. It was a great start to our relationship.

It may have been, but aside from the whip ban, there was another immediate concern, as Charlie had to dismount Trapper John shortly after the finish of the race after he feared the horse had broken down. 'He had actually hit a nerve in his knee and went lame for a few strides, but he was sound afterwards and actually ran at Aintree two weeks later where he was second by just half a length to Jimmy Fitzgerald's Sip Of Orange in the Oddbins Hurdle over 3m 1f,' Cummins remembers.

After a hiatus of nearly a year due to injury between 24 November 1990 (when he beat Bradbury Star at Newbury) and 16 November 1991 (when he returned to finish a distant ninth in the Sean Graham Brown Lad Handicap Hurdle behind Linvar) he was back on track for Cheltenham.

However there was an unpleasant ending to Trapper John's attempt to regain his Stayer's Hurdle title in 1992 when, after finishing three and a half lengths behind Barry Hills' Nomadic Way, he was disqualified when Swan failed to draw the correct weight at weighing-in. 'To this day we don't know what happened. Charlie weighed in threes pounds light, but we just don't know what happened. He had definitely weighed-out at the right weight. There was no impropriety on anyone's behalf and we still don't understand what happened,' Cummins says.

Mouse himself says that he had 'absolutely no doubt' where the fault lay:

They weighed him out incorrectly – no doubt. I retraced all my steps, from where we had saddled the horse to where I gave Charlie the leg-up, and I found no lead anywhere. There was no hole in the lead pocket so, unless there was a real good pickpocket there on the day, I have no doubt that the Clerk of the Scales cocked up. No doubt at all. Ever since though, I always go to the scales just to be sure to be sure. I was like a dog over it, because it was as much embarrassing as it was frustrating.

The horse actually ran again the following day in the Coral Golden Hurdle Final, but struggled to finish thirteenth behind My View, trained by Tommy Stack. He was next seen at the end of that month at Ascot where he was beaten by half a length by Martin Pipe's Pragada in the Letheby and Christopher Long Distance Hurdle.

He would run only twice more in his career and did not win again before being retired. Trapper John still lives at Everardsgrange, happy in his retirement at the ripe old age of twenty-four.

11 Lean Times: Keeping the Show on the Road

While the majority of observers would speak favourably of Mouse's training abilities, there was one side to the business that he was never any good at – the financial side. He coldly admits as much himself – and it was to be very late in his career before the money problems eased off:

> Back in the early days the prize money was shit and I can honestly say it has only been in recent years that I've actually made a profit on the books. In fact I don't know how many times I've been told to give it up. In recent times we've been asset-rich but cash-poor, but at least there is something now to leave to the two boys. I've had sheriffs in here, the taxman – we've been through the mill.

Timmy Hyde says that the racing industry is a like a roller coaster at the best of times – training in particular – but he feels that Mouse has had a wilder rides than most: 'He's been through some very lean times and it has been tough for him and he has had to be tough too, but he has come through and it's been great in more recent times for him to be able to prove that if he has the material, he can do the business. But it has been a rollercoaster, no doubt.'

There are those that might surmise that because his father is a lord, Mouse may have benefited from father's largesse: the truth of the matter is that Lord Killanin was never a seriously rich man and never had the sort of wealth that would support a training operation which was occasionally beset by major financial crises of one sort or another.

Shanny has already pointed out that in the very early days both their families were very supportive, but Mouse agrees that, while this was the case on a small scale, the support from his mother and father was no more than that:

> The old man was not a rich man, even if he did make lots of money for other people. I can assure you, there were never any handouts there … that was not the way of it. At one point I got screwed by an accountant down in Limerick who left me rightly in the shit. He was supposed to have everything in order, but the only thing he looked after was himself. After that I had to get everything refinanced again. You have to remember that when I was broke up with my leg, I had nothing coming in and times were very tough indeed. The time the sheriff arrived, I remember he was very apologetic about it because he reckoned the people in the Revenue wanted to send out a message to the racing community about keeping their books in order – PAYE and PRSI and all that – and I was the one they made an example of. I was the one they picked on.

Ted Walsh can empathise with the sort of financial obstacles that Mouse ran into over the years and he says bluntly:

> Most trainers die paupers. There is barely a living in training horses. There's no pension, no fall-back – no nothing. Training racehorses, for the great majority, is financial suicide. Fellas end up as jockeys in their early thirties and, while some can go back to the family farm or they become bloodstock agents, if you haven't got that and you love horses, the natural progression is to go training. Look at someone like Fred Winter who was Champion Jockey a half-a-dozen times in England and when he gave up he actually wanted to become a starter. But the powers-that-be wouldn't allow him to become a starter and so, from having nothing better to do, he became a trainer. He was hugely successful, as we know, but he still ended up penniless.
>
> Most fellas who train never got a degree in fucking economics or anything and they sit down and work out what it is roughly – very roughly – going to cost. They may have a property they bought

during their riding career but when they start training they have all sorts of other costs – wages, staff, rent and rates and all that. They have not been educated to cope with these costs and for most fellas they have to deal in horses to survive. The downside of that is that you're selling off your best animals. The fellas who become successful are flat trainers who train big numbers and who win classic races with top quality horses.

Any fella who starts off training has to be conservative with what he charges because if he charges too much people will say, 'Sure, look at so-and-so down the road who's an established trainer and he's not charging any more than that.' So, in order to be some way competitive, you end up charging a bit less than most and that few quid less is the suicide route. Throw in the cost of building gallops and all that stuff and you realise that training really is financial suicide.

Even in his early days Mouse would have had support from people because they felt honour-bound to do so. Look at Mrs Valentine, for example. She would have felt that because he got crocked riding her horse in America, she was duty-bound to support him as a trainer. They would be the sort of people – a bit like Betty Moran [owner of Grand National winner, Papillon] has been for me – who would never pull the plug. They were always going to have horses with him.

This theme is reinforced by Tony Mullins, who says that the training game is nothing like as lucrative as most people seem to think it is:

I haven't got the exact figures from the Trainers' Association, but I think something like sixty per cent of people who have a training licence today will not have a training licence in five years time. Years ago I fought with the authorities to get a jockeys' pension and I have also been doing the same to try and get something similar organised for trainers. But the amazing thing about trainers is that they can rarely agree on anything and they will not stick together. It was something I was passionate about, but I failed. Couldn't get them to agree; jockeys can work together, owners will work together – but not trainers.

Whatever about the largely devoted support he has enjoyed from his owners down the years, Liam Burke recalls a man who was never worried by impending financial disasters: 'Once he had a boiled egg, a cup of coffee and a fag in the mornings, nothing bothered him. Although he'd panic in the mornings if he couldn't find a cigarette – he could do nothing without them.'

Bob Townend was one of the first people to ride for Mouse and he arrived at Everardsgrange having been a stable jockey to Mick O'Toole on the Curragh for nearly ten years. He would be associated with the Fethard yard for several years, both as a jockey and head lad, and he recalls that while the basic facilities were there in the initial years, they were fairly rudimentary and, more often than not, things were very tight:

> It was quite hand-to-mouth at times and I can remember times when people in Fethard would not be too keen on changing a wages cheque for you, but you always got paid. I remember one morning when there were a pile of big lorries in the yard when we came to work and I remember thinking that maybe the BBC had come down to film the place or something. But when I got closer I realised it wasn't the BBC, it was the sheriff! But he always seemed to be always able to tough it out – light a Major and carry on.

Smoking was – and still is – an integral part of the Mouse Morris persona and Liam maintains that Mouse 'couldn't do anything without a cigarette.' Burke also reckons he has more insights than most into just how thin things got in those early days:

> We never, ever failed to get paid, no matter how tight it was. Mouse was, and is, a great man with horses, but he hadn't a clue about business. His problem was that he'd go and do one thing and then he'd go and do something else before he was financially sorted for the first one. I used to see bills coming in there and you'd wonder how they'd be paid, but they were. Himself and Shanny used to do the books before they got someone in to try and do a proper job.
>
> The bottom line was that when he had a good horse, he knew what to do with it. He might have been even better if he wasn't off hunting so often, but he did very well with what he had in the really early days because there were not too many good horses kept in the country back then.

Johnny Cummins spent the longest time as head lad at the yard, joining shortly after Buck House had died in such tragic circumstances and remaining for twenty-one years. He admits:

> That wasn't a great time to have joined him, because things were at such a low ebb. I was just a lad at the time and I remember looking after the likes of Trapper John and Cahervillahow in my early days there. We had some great days with those horses, but there were some very quiet times in the years that immediately followed. I remember a time when we had maybe only twenty-one or twenty-two horses and, while Mouse always wanted more quality than quantity, things looked very bleak at times.

He says that although money was sometimes tight there were never any fears among the staff about getting paid at the end of the week:

> You'd know, by times, when there were strange cars coming into the yard that there were guys after him for money, but we always got paid on a Friday. There were never any issues with the staff on that front. Maybe when there were a lot of empty boxes you might have wondered how he was keeping it all together, particularly when he was keeping the same level of staff on board, but we always got our wages.

Liam Burke was there long before Johnny Cummins and he makes no bones about the fact that there were times when things at Everardsgrange were distinctly hand-to-mouth:

> What mystified me was that he *should* have had money, but what was he doing with it? He wasn't gambling and he wasn't pissing it up. In the heel of the hunt though, no matter how tight things got, we never failed to get paid. Never. He might have owed money all around him, but we always got paid.

Mouse himself admits to being a bad businessman but he maintains that there was often a force majeure in what was going on and he was forced to write off monies owed to him by other people and this was what got him into hot water. Having had a bad experience with an accountant did not help and the politically motivated visit of the sheriff had nothing to do with him, but was aimed as a warning shot to the racing community in general. He also points out that things could not have been that bad if he was able to hang on to his house and his property. Many others in Ireland of the 1980s were not able to do so.

Mouse might never have endeared himself to his creditors, but the loyalty he engendered in owners and staff, as well as his inherent abilities as a trainer, always saw him through. And another Cheltenham winner could only add to his burgeoning reputation. It would not be far off.

12 Methodology: Working for the Mouse

Tommy Carmody, stable jockey in Mouse's early training years, maintains that Mouse was always a very easy man to work with because of his background as a jockey and that this gave him a very sympathetic approach to the perils race-riders face: 'Having come from the riding side of things, he understood that horses make mistakes and that jockeys make mistakes too and he was able to differentiate between the two. He could obviously read a race better than most people because he had been a jockey, but he would know what might have happened in a race before you came in and told him.'

By the time he arrived at Everardsgrange, Carmody had already won a Champion Chase (on Hilly Way) as well as three consecutive King George V Chases (on Gay Spartan and twice on Silver Buck) and was a seasoned and successful campaigner but, oddly, he cannot remember if he was on a retainer when he came to Fethard: 'I don't recall if he ever paid me at all,' he quips, continuing:

> It was a small yard back then – I suppose it still is in a way – but he had really good owners, the Magniers, the O'Reillys and so forth, and it was a good place for me to be then.
>
> What I liked about him was that he would never tie you down with unnecessary instructions. He would tell you what he thought and then let you get on with it. Working with Mouse was a very happy time for me professionally, and eventually when we parted it was on the best of terms.
>
> He was always a laid-back character and he just rolled with

whatever punches came at him. He has done tremendously well for himself and one thing you can be sure of is that if he had a horse good enough to go to Cheltenham, it always got there in tip-top shape. His horses always come to the fore at Cheltenham.

Carmody, famously and almost uniquely among top National Hunt jockeys, never broke a bone in his body during a long and illustrious career until a crashing fall at Naas in 1991 resulted in a condition known to medical people as 'frozen shoulder'.

'I'd have been better off if I broke the shoulder, but I didn't and in the end – after a year of keyhole surgery and other treatment – the authorities would not renew my licence and that was the end of it,' he says matter-of-factly.

Ted Walsh also rode a lot for Mouse as an amateur and he reckons he was an easy guy to ride for, particularly as he'd been there himself. 'He knows what he wants and he knows his horses. Also, he knows that if something goes arseways it's not always your fault. He's an easy fella to ride for and he always seems to be able to get the best out of his horses on the big days.'

It was a dashing young jockey called Charlie Swan who took up the reins as Mouse's retained jockey in the wake of Carmody's departure, steering Trapper John to Cheltenham success in 1990. The son of trainer Captain Dermot Swan, whose licence he would eventually take over when his own riding career ended, Charlie was born into racing and, like Mouse, knew he wanted to be a jockey from an early age. He was apprenticed to flat legend Kevin Prendergast initially, before his weight got to him and he went National Hunt racing with Dessie Hughes at Osborne Lodge on the Curragh.

His impact on the scene was such that, when Carmody left Everards-grange to take up a job with John Mulhern, Mouse turned to Swan to replace him. Swan remembers:

That was 1988 or 1989, I would say, and part of the attraction for me was that I knew he had a lot of good owners and the chances were that he would find good horses for them. When you're a young fella you're always hoping that you'll come across good horses and I did when I went there.

Mouse was always a guy who liked to have his own jockey and I must say I'd be the same now. In that situation you have someone who'll look after the horses because he'll be riding them the next day as well. They're not going to beat the shit out of them because they know there will be other days. With National Hunt horses they can stay racing until they are twelve or thirteen – or even longer – so you have to look after them. It is only natural for a jockey who knows he's not going to be riding a horse ever again to try and get the best out of them, but that's not always good for the horse. You can see why he'd want a regular first jockey.

When Swan moved to Everardsgrange, Hughes was going through a nightmare period of virus in his yard and the jockey honestly confesses that he 'couldn't see a lot of winners coming', so he was keen for a change of scene. As he says:

A jump jockey has only got a short career and you have to make the most of it. At that time he had horses like Mixed Blends, which was second in the Supreme Novices, and Trapper John was second in the SunAlliance Novices' Hurdle, so I knew they would be there. Caher-villahow was also coming good back then and Lastofthebrownies was going to be a horse I could ride in the Grand National.

The relationship between the pair was a very fruitful one and Swan remembers it with fondness:

He had an empathy with jockeys and there was never any shouting and roaring out of him. I never got a bollocking off him, but then I'd say that was because I never gave one of his a bad ride! Even when there were bad times or when decisions went against you, he was always very phlegmatic. And even when you could reasonably expect him to go mad, he was always very calm and kept the head. He never gave out to me or he never said things to the press and that can take a fair amount of control.

Pretty much everyone gets on with Mouse because he's a real nice fella and he's very easy to get on with. He's a very quiet guy and he's also a very good loser and in racing you have to be because you lose more often than you win. But, from a jockey's point of view, the very fact that he ate, slept and drank thinking about winning at Cheltenham was very positive because I was the same.

Now a trainer of some note himself, Swan says the biggest thing he probably picked up from Mouse was the fact that he doesn't 'run the shit out of the horses'. He also liked the fact that, as stable jockey, Mouse did not insist on having him down to Fethard every day and 'only really wanted to see your face when he wanted a specific piece of work done' with a horse. 'There was no time-wasting, he only got you there when he wanted you.'

Swan recounts that he and Mouse never fell out, rather that the trainer simply went away and got someone else 'when I wasn't riding the ones he wanted me to ride.'

Conor O'Dwyer was also stable jockey at Everardsgrange and, from a rider's point of view, he feels Mouse was an ideal man to work for:

> One great thing about Mouse was that once you got to the parade ring there were no added instructions. The plan of the race is laid down beforehand and he reckons that when they get to the parade ring he's done his job and now it's time for you to do yours. OK, he'll give you a pointer or two, but he won't be telling you to 'be here' or 'be there' or whatever – that is your job. I'm sure that comes from his experience as a jockey.
>
> I know from my experience as a jockey that if a trainer gives you instructions that tie you down, then you can end up in trouble. Sure, things will change during the course of a race and you have to use your own intuition, but it is nice not to be tied down. If you're a good enough jockey you should know what to do and what's what; that's Mouse's theory on it. When it does go wrong, as long as you're man enough to come in and admit you messed up, but that the horse is in great form, Mouse will always be fine with that.

O'Dwyer, having ridden his last race at Cheltenham in March 2007, is just beginning a new career as a trainer and he says he has learned plenty from Mouse over the years:

> He had a lot of owners over the years who were not there very often and that gave him a chance to assess the horses realistically and if they were not up to scratch then they were out. It worked for him and it worked for me there too. He probably has the right idea

because some people are happy to have their hundred horses, or whatever, but they have to know that most of them only might win a race.

Mouse always wanted to have horses that will win races. Maybe a lot of trainers cannot do it financially, but I think that if you have the owners, it is a great way of working this business. I'm going training now and I'd certainly like to do it that way too. You can keep the numbers small, the staff levels small and the quality high, both in terms of owners and horses.

He has always been highly thought of and, unlike some people, he is not at all pushy. There are lads out there who would give their right arm to have some of Mouse's owners. These sort of people don't grow on trees. But the bottom line is that it has always been his business and he runs it the way he sees fit. The other side of the coin, though, is that he keeps those owners happy. He had never got owners under false pretences either, because he's shown consistently he's able to do the job.

I hope in my training career I will be as brave with owners when it comes to telling them to cut their losses because their horse is not going to win. The other side of it, too, is that horses can make a liar out of you most days of the week, but decent owners like that sort of honesty. With syndicates you can get a situation where they don't believe what they are being told and they move the horse on to the next guy, but that doesn't happen with decent owners. And the thing about Mouse is that there are very few examples of where a horse he thought was useless turned out to be anything else.

On top of that, he has always had a good team of lads down there in Everardsgrange and most of them have been with him a long time. He trusts his staff: they are part of the team and he listens to what they have to say.

Others who have plenty to say are those who have worked as head lad at Everardsgrange over the years, such as Bob Townend who says that, right from the get-go as a trainer, Mouse always wanted his own jockey in the yard:

He wanted fellas who knew the horses and knew what to do with them in racing circumstances. He always felt having his own man in the yard was essential because once they knew the horses, he didn't have to be too specific with instructions. He worked on the basis that they would know themselves what to do in any given situation. He's had to battle back from a few times when things didn't look good, but in recent years all the boxes have been full and mostly with really nice horses.

Another former head lad, Johnny Cummins, reckons that, horses aside, Mouse also always attracted good staff, even in thin times:

> He's been lucky to have had nice, genuine people down through the years, but I suppose a good man will always attract good staff. He was never one to shout and roar and, while he might lose the head a bit on the gallops sometimes if someone did something wrong, his reaction was usually the opposite to what you'd expect. Instead of shouting, he might say nothing at all and sometimes that's worse.

Having started as just a normal lad in the yard, Cummins was promoted to the position of travelling head lad when Sean Devanney moved out of that job to become head lad. After six years in that job and a year before he married his wife, Lynn, Johnny himself became head lad and held that position until April 2007, when he left to set up his own pre-training and livery operation.

His departure was actually marked live on national television in Ireland during the 2007 Punchestown meeting, when Ted Walsh sent him the best wishes of the RTÉ crew in his new endeavour. Cummins reckons that the pair 'never had a cross word' during all their years together and he commends his former boss as being 'a sound man to work for.'

Liam Burke, now a renowned trainer and winner of the 2007 Galway Plate with Sir Frederick, was one of the first employees Mouse hired when he started his training career and the circumstances surrounding his arrival at Everardsgrange involved something of a misfortune for the Corkman: 'I was working here [at what was his parents' home near Conna and what is now his own training base] and I had about seven cattle stolen on me and I had to go and find work of some description. They were all we had at the time and I needed money.'

Through neighbour and then stable jockey to Mouse, Bob Townend, he ended up travelling to Fethard to ride out at the yard. 'It was September 1981 and I met Mouse in Listowel and he told me to come on up and I went up with Bob, thinking it would only last a few weeks. Maurice Eddon was the head lad there then but he left and I was offered the job. I was there for four years.'

He recalls that one of the best horses Mouse ever had, in his opinion, was a small horse called Key Largo:

> Sean Devanney (then travelling head lad) and myself were the only two that knew about him the first time he went racing. Sean used to ride Hi Harry out and he was a good horse too. The first day they worked together, Key Largo wasn't able for Harry at all, but the last day they worked, he was well able for him. This was just before Killarney and there was a gamble on, without a doubt, but someone fucked it up because he was 8/1 before racing and someone took the price. It ruined a good touch for the rest of us. I had a few bob on him, but I only got 5/2. It also cost me a friend because Ferdy Murphy, who was training for the Durcans at the time, had asked me about our horse and I'd told him that it had no chance. He wasn't very impressed when our fella pissed in. Hi Harry had run there the same day and we'd have been on for a right double, only that someone blabbed about Key Largo and the price vanished.
>
> He also had a fierce troublesome horse called Leggit, who was owned by John Horgan. By Jaysus he made some job of him. He was a real handful and he was a horse that had to be really fresh before he'd run. I remember that if a vet came near the place, he'd climb the walls and wouldn't let him near the stable. He could smell them coming.

Burke also saw a side of the trainer that many people don't get to see and he uses to examples to illustrate the fact:

> He had a Dobermann called Trouble and I remember when he died it was the only time I saw Mouse cry. He was a terrible bastard of

a dog actually, because he used to sit on the circle on the gallops and
he'd jump up at the horses when they passed by. He dropped three
of us one day. That red BMW – ZIM 777, I'll never forget it – saw
a lot of action one day when Trouble started hunting the horses on
the gallops and Mouse took off after him in the car around the
field. He reckoned he was doing forty mph around the field after
the dog. The dog was killed afterwards when one of the neighbours
pulled into the yard and knocked him down. Mouse was distraught.

I remember another time when Mouse nearly lost his reason.
One of the local lads who'd just come to us from school – he was
only sixteen or so - was riding a horse belonging to the Horgans
called First Banquet. They had had him training on the flat with
Richard Hannon before he came to Mouse and he was a bit messy
to ride. Anyway the young fella got frustrated with the horse and
he flicked the reins at him. But didn't he catch the horse in the eye
and took it straight out of his head. Mouse went absolutely mental
and I can't say he was wrong. The horse spent several weeks at the
Troytown Hospital after and it took him a long time to adjust to
having only the one eye. Even so, he won a hurdle race afterwards.
But it was the only time I ever really saw Mouse boiling mad, and
I wouldn't blame him.

Bob Townend has varied memories too:

I remember one day when Lastofthebrownies won the Munster
National in Limerick and I was there representing Mouse. After the
race the press guys asked me where Mouse was and I said that he
was out hunting. He was not impressed – in fact he was livid –
when he read that in the paper the following day and he told me
never to say that again. He told me that in future I was to say that
he was 'entertaining owners'.

He also had a horse at one stage called Decent Prospect and I'd
say that he was one of the best he ever had. One night Mouse went
out to give the horses a final look-over before going to bed and
somehow the horse had injured himself. I'd say he might even have
been the best horse Mouse has ever trained because you couldn't
get another horse to work with him at home – he'd just destroy
them. But, unfortunately, he was never the same horse again and

even though John Halley did a fantastic job of stitching him up, he was never right. We never found out what had happened him – whether it was dogs had chased him or what – but I remember that was a very low time.

I remember, too, one time when he [Mouse] had just laid down a new gallop and something happened that the whole thing was washed away. It was washed nearly into Fethard. It had cost him a fortune to get the thing put in and then it was just washed away. Those things are sent to try you, but there is always the balancing factor of the joy of having a winner at Cheltenham. We saw lots of up and downs.

Liam Burke has a clear recollection of the same incident:

Eimear Haughey [daughter of late Taoiseach Charles Haughey] used to ride out there some mornings and she even had a horse or two with Mouse. Anyway, she arrived one morning and it was after a savage flood and one of the pipes in the yard got blocked and the water ran down the gallop and took the whole lot off and washed it away. Eimear arrived in the same morning, bright as a button: 'Hi Mouse, I just met your gallop down the road!'

The likes of Cummins, Burke and Townend have long since moved on to other things, but their memories and those of the jockeys that rode for Mouse all have a common thread – there are few, if any, bad words to be found. Sure there were bad times and certainly there were great highs too, but their fondness for Mouse and their good memories of time with him is universal. Not too many horse trainers can boast that sort of endorsement.

13 Cahervillahow: The Unluckiest of Horses

Charlie Swan was at the centre of one of the most controversial events of Mouse Morris' career when he was aboard Cahervillahow at Sandown on 27 April 1991 and rode him to win the Whitbread Gold Cup, but was subsequently disqualified in contentious circumstances.

It was a decent renewal of the race, with two runners each from Martin Pipe and Nicky Henderson (Omerta and Bonanza Boy for the former, Ten Of Spades and Won't Be Gone Long for the latter), while Kim Bailey had Docklands Express and David Barons sent out the fancied Seagram, who would win the Grand National the following year.

Mrs Valentine's Cahervillahow and Docklands Express started joint favourites at 4/1, with Seagram and Omerta at 9/2 and 6/1 respectively. History records that Cahervillahow won by three-quarters of a length from Docklands Express, but was disqualified when Swan was adjudged to have interfered with the second horse on the run-in.

The 'comments in running' in the *Racing Post* state that Cahervillahow 'led last, hung right, driven out (finished first, disqualified and placed second).' The same source tells us that Docklands Express 'led approaching last, soon headed, carried right flat, ran on (finished second three-quarters of a length, awarded race).'

To many observers the outcome was nothing short of a massive injustice because, while Swan had admittedly drifted across the course and carried his opponent with him, there was little doubt that there was no interference and at no time did Anthony Tory have to stop riding

Docklands Express. The stewards felt otherwise, however, and Caher-villahow lost the race. Swan remembers the day vividly:

> It was absolutely terrible and, while Mouse was bitterly disappointed, he never gave out to me and he never said much in the press, although a lot of other trainers would have. It takes a fair amount of self-control in such circumstances not to lose the head; I know a lot of people who would have lost the plot if they were in a similar position – and possibly felt righteous about it as well.

The loss of the Whitbread was not the only bizarre incident in the career of this very talented but seemingly jinxed horse, and Swan is readily able to list some of the disasters that befell Cahervillahow:

> He was one unlucky horse. He was beaten a short head in the Irish Grand National; he was second in the Thyestes; second in the big handicap at Cheltenham, the Ritz Club Handicap; second in the infamous voided Grand National won by Esha Ness; and then he won the Whitbread and was disqualified. The list seemed endless.
>
> Getting beat a short head in the Irish National was a real sickener. It was just so close and when you get beaten by such a small margin in such a big race it affects you more than it might otherwise.
>
> The thing about the Whitbread was that I was fairly sure there would be an inquiry because I did bring the horse across. But, if you look at all the videos of the race over the years at Sandown, all the horses do that. It has something to do with the contours of the place, but all the horses drift that way – out away from the stand rail towards the inner.
>
> The other jockey didn't stop riding at all but, like an eejit, I probably made a mistake by sitting up when I felt I had him beat. I won by over half a length. Had I won a length and a half, or two lengths, there might not have been a problem. When I had him beat I started looking over at him and that might have made the difference. Whatever, I definitely thought I'd keep the race.
>
> The Whitbread is one of very few meetings where there are jumps and flat racing on the same card and I often wonder if we were disqualified because there were flat stewards on duty that day.

Racing tight on the flat is a bit different than going three and a half miles over fences. It was all very disappointing, but Mouse was very good about it. He was great the way he never lost his cool and never went mad in the press.

The two of us knew, going over for the appeal, that we had no chance: they were not going to reverse the decision. We thought that appealing the original decision was the right thing to do, but we knew that it was only very rarely a decision like that is overturned. Even so, we thought we had to lodge the appeal – for our own peace of mind as much as anything. But the establishment rarely admits its own men are wrong. You can see the way it works, but in this instance it was very unfortunate that I had to be on the receiving end of it.

Mouse himself today admits that he is still disbelieving that the race was taken from his horse:

We won it fair and square but, for whatever reason, they decided to take it off us. I don't think any racing person who saw the race could believe what they did, but the history book shows that we were disqualified and that's that. We did appeal, but we knew we'd no chance. We appealed in the hope that natural justice might be applied, but we knew in our heart of hearts going over there for the hearing that they would not change the result. After two minutes inside that room, we definitely knew we'd no chance.

However there was one small crumb of comfort for Mouse after the initial decision to disqualify his horse from first place. As he was kicking his heels in the weigh room, a bowler-hatted gentleman approached him and said, 'Mr Morris, would you mind, the Queen Mother would like to meet you.'

Mouse was duly trotted upstairs to meet the late Queen Mother and he recalls that she was very nice and very sympathetic: 'She didn't say in so many words that she was sorry I had been done out of the race, or anything, but she complimented me on what a nice horse I had and wished me the very best for the future. I suppose she felt sorry for me, but it was nice of her to ask to meet me.'

According to Ted Walsh, who is never afraid to venture an opinion on such matters – a fact which has made him one of the most popular and incisive of racing's television pundits – the decision to take the Whitbread from Mouse's horse was the 'second worst' decision he has ever seen on a racecourse in his long career:

> The worst I ever saw was when James Fanshawe's horse, Royal Gait, was disqualified from the Ascot Gold Cup after he interfered with another horse about a mile out from the winning post. Cash Asmussen rode him that day and they took the race off him. He actually won five or six lengths and that was the worst decision I've ever seen. The one in which Mouse's horse was disqualified was the second worst.
>
> Cahervillahow was caught out because at Sandown the whole track drifts towards the inner. The final fence is under the stand and the finish becomes a sort of a funnel. But the thing was that he never interfered with the other horse at all. It was pure and utter robbery. Nobody can fathom why they took the race from him. I remember saying at the time that I thought it was daylight robbery and to this day my opinion has not changed. The fella who came to the decision had to be either drunk, blind, or have had a good few quid on the second horse.

In the wake of the Whitbread disqualification Mouse received letters from all over Britain and Ireland from people expressing their disgust at the decision. He actually went to the trouble of getting them all mounted and framed and they still hang on the wall of his office at Everardsgrange. 'Some of them were only addressed to "Mouse Morris, Ireland" and they got to me,' the trainer muses.

Johnny Cummins says that not only was Mouse 'gutted' after the Whitbread, but that the whole yard was devastated:

> The thing was that Mouse was not even sure of running him in the Whitbread because it came after the defeat in the Irish National. But the horse was very well in himself and it was decided to give him his chance. What happened after was a real sickener. Everyone knows that it was a great injustice.
>
> He was an unlucky horse, very unlucky. He was a bit of a hyper horse and it was hard to keep condition on him, but he never had

a scrap of luck. He fell on the road when he was a young horse and the year when he was beaten in the Irish National, he was also narrowly beaten in the Ritz at Cheltenham. He reared up at the start of that race and he was pushed out to the outside and [Peter] Scudamore kept pushing him out at every fence and he was beaten by five lengths by Seagram, with Garrison Savannah back in third.

For his part, Mouse is quite phlegmatic, even at this remove: 'You cannot rationalise something like the ill-fortune that dogged Cahervillahow, you just have to drive on. You have to take it on the chin because there is nothing else you can do. If he was finishing last all the time that would be one thing, but getting beat a short head all the time at least shows you were doing something right with the bloody horse.'

If those in the yard could not believe the misfortune that seemed to dog their horse, then they would have to suspend disbelief even further the following year when Cahervillahow was mistakenly taken out of the Gold Cup entries due to an unfortunate clerical error. That Gold Cup was won by Garrison Savannah – whom he had beaten at Cheltenham – and all concerned were left scratching their heads and wondering if Mrs Valentine's horse could have been their first winner of chasing's Blue Riband. They would have to wait awhile to realise that dream.

14 Fallow Years

Other trainers might reflect warmly on the pleasure of training excellent horses, but for Mouse Morris the absence of big race winners – particularly at Cheltenham or Aintree – is almost painful. Even if the horses are winning big prizes at home in Ireland, his whole raison d'être is compromised if horses fail to deliver a win when they are sent to England. Among the horses in those years – including the likes of His Song, Boss Doyle, Foxchapel King, What A Question, Keepatem and Cahervillahow – there were many minor stars, but none really served to fuel Mouse's Cheltenham dreams.

His Song was second in a Supreme Novices' Hurdle and had nine career wins, as well as amassing total career earnings approaching £150,000 for his owner David Lloyd, the former British Davis Cup captain and hugely successful leisure tycoon. Interestingly, the horse made second to French Ballerina in the Citroen Supreme Novices, ridden by future flat star, Richard Hughes (son of Dessie); while none other than A. P. McCoy won on the horse a little over a month later at Punchestown in the Country Pride Champion Novices' Hurdle, fighting back on the run-in to defeat French Ballerina by a head. However ultimately he did not add to Mouse's Cheltenham tally and, in the trainer's own mind, that made him a failure.

The diminutive Foxchapel King, owned by ever-loyal supporter Tony O'Reilly, was also hugely successful in his own right, earning £308,000 during his seven-year career and winning some huge prizes along the way, including the Troytown at Navan and the Intervet Trophy at Cheltenham's November meeting. However, he never made that step up from being a good horse to being a great one and he was another for whom Mouse had once dreamed great things without seeing them fulfilled.

Between 23 November 1996 and 30 April 1998, Vincent Daly's Boss Doyle put together a remarkable string of results in which he was only once out of the first two in thirteen outings – the exception being an extremely disappointing eleventh in the Royal and SunAlliance Novices' Hurdle in March 1997, behind the legendary Istabraq. He amassed nearly £170,000 in earnings during his career, but once more never truly cracked the big time.

Conor O'Dwyer, Mouse's stable jockey during these years, also remembers big race wins for the likes of Keepatem and What A Question:

> What A Question [winner of some £140,000 in career earnings] was a real tough filly. She was not over-burdened with ability, but she had the heart of a lion. I won a good few races on her and she was third in a stayer's [to Cyborgo in 1996], and won a good few chases afterwards.
>
> Keepatem [who won £151,000 in total prize money for owner J. P. McManus] was another horse that was there during my second stint with Mouse and he won the Paddy Power Chase at Leopardstown [on 27 December 2004, from Jaquouille, landing a massive gamble in the process]. That was a great bit of training because he was a small horse and it was hard to get him right in the weights. Mouse definitely got him right that day and he won with 10st 7lbs on his back.

Indeed, the *Racing Post* noted at the time that this was:

> ... a triumph for Mouse Morris, as the heavily backed Keepatem took advantage of a rating that was widely perceived as giving him an excellent chance in only his second handicap chase. Stamina is the key to him and he got a nerveless ride from Conor O'Dwyer who threaded him through the field from four out to get into serious contention off the home turn. He led just after the last and kept on strongly to give his owner a second successive victory in the race. This was an object lesson in strategic planning by his connections.

New Co was another Paddy Power winner for the Mouse–O'Dwyer team several years earlier in 1996, but that was a time when the jockey was also riding a lot for Christy Roche and J. P. McManus and could not commit fully to the Everardsgrange outfit, allowing Shay Barry and David Casey to come in and ride horses like His Song and Foxchapel King.

Charlie Swan, who took over from O'Dwyer at Everardsgrange, remembers Lastofthebrownies being one of the horses in Mouse's yard that attracted him in the first place:

> Lastofthebrownies was a super ride for the Grand National, but it was just unfortunate that the ground came up to quick the year he ran. It was flat out the whole way that year and, while he was usually a horse who'd travel in a race and you'd be pulling on him, this time he was always off the bridle and it was balls out all the way. He jumped brilliant, but I could never get him into a challenging position because when I went to ask him for a last effort there was no more there to be got.

Revisiting these horses with Mouse is a fairly matter-of-fact experience:

> They just weren't up to scratch. Sure Boss Doyle was a good horse, but he wasn't a *great* horse and the same applied to most of the rest of them. It was just brilliant training that got the most out of them [he laughs]. Sure they were all in the money on a regular basis, but the fact is that they were not up to the top standard and that's why none of them won the really big races or performed at Cheltenham. But in this business you console yourself all the time. I had had three separate winners at Cheltenham by then and there were plenty of trainers out there who'd never even had one. So you count your blessings.

★

During this period, too, the relationship between Mouse and Shanny began to unravel completely. What had begun so many years previously with an infatuation that caused Mouse to fly to Australia to snare the beautiful girl from Kilmacanogue, County Wicklow, eventually imploded.

It is not a subject Mouse likes to talk about much, but close friend and supporter, Alfie Buller, remembers a time when life became hell for the Master of Everardsgrange.

'Shanny adored Mouse', he says, 'and I think she just got frustrated that there was never any money.' Buller reckons that Shanny tried various things to rectify the situation but it never seemed to work out and there was always another crisis to be faced. Ultimately – but only after a lot of trauma and recrimination – the couple split. Buller maintains:

> She was a gorgeous girl, but I was always very supportive of both of them. Shanny was – and is – a very good friend, but Mouse found it hard to cope with her leaving. It devastated him when she left. If you are a sportsman – and he is, above everything else – and your game has turned to shit, then your life turns to shit too. He has been to hell and back and any bit of sunshine he gets, he has paid the price for it in hell. A lot of people would say that it wasn't really hell, just a fucked-up marriage or whatever, but to Mouse it was much different. He was deeper than most people credited him for and it affected him greatly.

That Shanny left after an Irish Grand National meeting was the straw that broke the camel's back. That she eventually returned turned out to be of little long-term significance, as the bonds of trust between the couple had been shattered and the relationship ultimately foundered.

A legal battle for custody of Christopher and Jamie was settled in their mother's favour and Mouse says it was one of the lowest days in his life when he stood outside Everardsgrange and watched his two boys being driven away, waving out the back window. It sparked, he says, a period in his life in which his focus vanished completely and his ability to concentrate on his job deserted him. He descended into a state of depression which still affects him to this day.

Mattie Ryan maintains that as Shanny and Mouse were two such disparate characters in any case, it was probably a miracle they got together in the first instance and also that their relationship lasted so long. 'It was probably odd for her to marry Mouse in the first place because she had no interest in horses. I don't know why she left in the end; maybe it was just that it was too difficult to live within the relationship. Whatever the reason, it affected him greatly.'

Mouse's brother Redmond, himself a divorcee, reckons that the time the couple split was very traumatic for his sibling:

That was an awful time for him – certainly the initial part of it – because it was not the easiest of splits. Having been in an amicable split myself – or at least as amicable a split as these things can be – I know these things are not easy. The other side of the coin is that I can't imagine Mouse being the easiest person to live with either, to be honest. He is pretty monosyllabic.

Watching from afar, long-time owner and supporter, John Horgan, maintains that Mouse may have sailed through unstable financial waters at times, but reckons that Shanny's departure was a real upset, because Mouse was so crazy about her – and, more pertinently, the children. 'That might have set him on a downer for a while because it might have upset his confidence or because his concentration wasn't there. But there were always people there who'd give him a horse when he needed one,' he says.

Alfie Buller reckons that Mouse had the support of his owners through thick and thin he says that is the case only because Mouse was an exceptional person:

> With regard to his financial problems, there was probably always enough security there to keep things afloat. Mouse probably just never was a businessman but, at the end of the day, if there were no room in life for the likes of Mouse Morris, the world would be a much lesser place. He is a special guy and I think that is first and foremost because he has a massive passion for the horse. He loves his horses. He is a competitive person also and he wants to win and he wants his horses to win and he wants them to win big races. Going to Tipperary, or somewhere like that on a Tuesday night would never give really light his fire. He is hungry for glory and that means he wants his horses to win at the really big meetings.
>
> He might have come from a privileged background, but there was no real money there and it was through horses he was able to express himself – as a jockey and as a trainer. His focus is only on winning on the big stage. There are very few people that would be as dedicated and as focused on just that one goal. For a lot of people the glory of having a horse is some day to have a good horse, but if they have a horse with Mouse and it is no good, his first advice will be to get out of it.

He illustrates the point with a typically pertinent story:

> A man came into my yard one time; he was seventy-eight years of age and he had brought a mare to a stallion. We'd had the lunch and we were walking out and I said to him: 'Why did you bother driving up – a five-hour drive up and another five hours back – why didn't you let us pick up the horse?' He put his arm around me and said: 'Alfred, there is nothing in life without a dream and the horse gives you the dream.' From my point of view there is no better man to share the dream with than the Mouse. He lives that dream every day of his life and, because of that, you would love to be the man that supports him to achieve the dream.
>
> But the problem is, I think, that Mouse has always been a bit too naive about people – he's too trusting. The fact of life is – for him – that people will probably always let you down, but a horse probably won't. Mouse has always trusted people more than he should.

In a minor financial crisis and in personal crises as well, things were not looking good for Mouse, and long-standing friend and owner of McCarthy's bar in Fethard, Annette McCarthy, highlights some of the problems that faced the trainer:

> Since Shanny left, he's been there on his own and he's such a shy man that he doesn't socialise much. He used to come here most evenings and he'd sit down the end of the bar there chatting with the lads with his glass of Smithwicks and a cigarette. But since the smoking ban came in he doesn't do that anymore. That ban destroyed him socially, which is awful.

Even as the smoking ban was taking hold, however, there were signs that Mouse had got his eye back on the Cheltenham ball. War Of Attrition was already coming through the ranks but, on 18 March 2005, the J. P. McManus-owned Fota Island won the Johnny Henderson Grand Annual Chase over two and a half miles at Prestbury Park, to become Mouse's fifth winner at the Festival meeting.

He landed a significant gamble that day when beating Bambi De L'Orme under a fine ride from Paul Carberry, and Frank Berry reckons that this was a fine training performance:

Fota Island's win was a great day and the horse never jumped better in his life. Mouse did a great job with him because, after he won at Cheltenham, he finished second in three Grade 1s the following year, including a second place behind Newmill in the Champion Chase. It was a big achievement to get him to that point, because he was only an ordinary jumper when he started.

As Mouse recalls:

To be honest, I thought he was useless when I got him first. He was by Supreme Leader and was a big, backward horse that was very slow to develop. But as time went on he got better and better and, in fairness, it was A. P. McCoy who pointed me in the direction of the Grand Annual. He rode him in Cork one day and when he came in he said we should definitely run him in that handicap. That was months beforehand and he was bang on.

In its analysis of the race, the *Racing Post* commented that this was a contest in which lightly weighted novices have a decent record and both Fota Island and Almaydan fitted the bill:

However, while Almaydan, grand sort that he is, had no pretensions to being other than a useful handicapper, Fota Island had been third in two Grade 1 hurdles last season, beaten only by Hardy Eustace and Rooster Booster at Punchestown on the second occasion, yet he was able to make his handicap debut over fences off a mark of only 130, despite racing from out of the handicap. Fota Island thus looked a possible blot on the weights and, whereas Almaydan was never really in contention and trailed home down the field, the winner's relative lack of experience was no obstacle and he travelled well. He was going really strongly as they came down the hill, his rider still biding his time, and once he was asked to go and win his race his biggest threat was a loose horse, whose attentions had become a real worry. Fota Island cleared away stylishly up the hill and ought to be capable of defying a much stiffer mark than this in due course. His next appearance is likely to be at Punchestown, where the target would presumably be back in novice company in the Swordlestown.

In actual fact, his next appearance was just three weeks after his Cheltenham victory, when Fota Island was sent to Aintree for the Red Rum Handicap Chase and defied a 12lb penalty for the Cheltenham win to beat Kadount, when ridden by A. P. McCoy. That partnership also stayed together for the following year's Champion Chase back at Cheltenham, when they finished second to Newmill in a race in which reigning champion, Moscow Flyer, and new-kid-on-the-block, Kauto Star, were among the most-fancied runners. Fota Island actually started the race as a 4/1 chance, while Kauto Star was the 2/1 favourite and the twelve-year-old Moscow Flyer was 5/1. Paul Nicholls' star novice fell at the third and Moscow Flyer was hampered in that incident, never really getting back into the race.

Newmill was the class of the field, landing a huge gamble for his west Cork connections and Fota Island was nine lengths back in second. It was not a bad start to a meeting that would eventually yield Mouse's greatest ever victory at Cheltenham.

It is said in Ireland that it is the *Rotha Mor an tSaoil* (the Great Wheel of Life) that controls life's cycle. If that is the case, redemption eventually comes to hand and all dreams come to fruition for those who work hardest for them. In Mouse's case it had taken time and effort and involved considerable frustration for the wheel to turn fully, but once he recovered focus after the trauma of separation, he would eventually nail the most prestigious prize in National Hunt racing.

15 It's War: Mouse Fights Back

The wider public may believe that winning the Grand National is the ultimate dream of everyone involved in National Hunt racing but for most of the cognoscenti, the Cheltenham Gold Cup is the prize they covet the most. They regard the Aintree classic as a pure lottery: a four-and-a-bit mile handicap that is more akin to open-air bingo than strategically planned horse-racing.

Mouse Morris is no different from most in the racing game in that regard. While he would willingly take a Grand National win if it were to pass his way, the dream of a Gold Cup is what it is all really about. This, after all, is a race for the best of the best jumpers in the business and only the best normally win it. However, there is one significant difference between Mouse and those that dream of a Gold Cup victory: he's actually done it.

His dream came true on 17 March (St Patrick's Day) 2006, when the seven-year-old War Of Attrition beat Willie Mullins' Hedgehunter and twenty other runners to win the Blue Riband of the steeplechase game. It was not a straightforward victory, however, as there were many twists and turns in the path of both trainer and horse on their way to this momentous result.

Mouse's very own replica of the famous Gold Cup trophy now sits proudly on the table in the dining-room at Everardsgrange and in pride of place just outside the front door of the house is the box inhabited by War Of Attrition – '2006 Cheltenham Gold Cup winner', as the inscribed plaque overhead proudly proclaims.

★

Like many good racing stories, this tale started in the most unpromising of circumstances. 'It's a brave man who'd persuade someone to buy a horse that fell in a point-to-point,' Timmy Hyde maintains. 'But Mouse saw him, saw something in him and picked him out.' He refers to the fact that Mouse had had his eye on this brown gelding – by Presenting, out of Una Juna, bred by Brid Murphy, born on 7 May 1999 and subsequently purchased as a three-year-old by Ger Hourigan at the Derby Sale at Fairyhouse – when he fell while twenty lengths in front at a point-to-point at Horse and Jockey in March 2003.

Hourigan himself remembers buying a horse that 'moved very nicely' and he says that Mouse, as well as Eddie and Michael O'Leary, had expressed interest in the horse before that point-to-point appearance: he was sold to the O'Learys within a week of that race.

Demi O'Byrne, himself no mean judge of a horse, maintains, 'it was not an accident that Mouse bought the Gold Cup winner', and he reckons that Mouse has an intuitive thing with horses – especially younger ones:

> It could not have been any other way because of his background. Some people have the gift and most haven't. There is no doubt that he soaked in an awful lot at both Nicholson's and at O'Grady's. On top of that, his record is extraordinary, but he is a very understated man and he never talks about how he does anything. I was very involved in the yard for a long time, from a vetinerary point of view, and I was there for the Buck House period and I have to say what he did with that horse was truly amazing. To achieve that sort of thing these days . . . [His voice trails off in admiration.]
>
> Not only did he have the knack of training horses right from the outset, but also he always had a view about how to get horses to Cheltenham and he became very successful at it. If you had a good horse, or you thought you had a good horse and you looked around to see who you'd get to train it, Mouse would be as good a person as there is in the world if you wanted a winner at Cheltenham. He also has the knack of giving a horse a long career, which is really what you need in this game. You rarely get a second chance, but he never needed it.

For his part, Ted Walsh recognises the fact that Mouse was very unlucky not to have picked up some really big pots with horses like Cahervilla-how, Boss Doyle and Foxchapel King in the years prior to War Of

Attrition's arrival in the yard and may, at this point, have felt frustrated that he was not enjoying the same sort of fortune which had decorated his earlier career. He comments:

> You can get to a stage where you have good horses, but they just don't win those races you'd like them to win. But I'd say Mouse got as good as there was to be got out of them. With a bit of luck he might have won one or two big ones, but you've got to take the swings with the roundabouts in this game. When War Of Attrition came along, I don't think many people in racing ever felt that Mouse had lost the ability to train a good horse and he duly went and proved it.

Ryanair boss Michael O'Leary has had a business career characterised by his ability to shred the rule book, but his eventual entrance into horse-racing was a lot more cautious than his business dealings, as the man himself relates:

> I grew up in Mullingar and my father always had a racehorse or two on the go. Generally he had a jumper or two, either through a syndicate or on his own. I was never really that interested, but my brother Eddie was and he found his way actively into the bloodstock industry by the age of about twenty and probably became one of the better pin-hookers in the country over time. I was always intrigued by jump racing and would usually go to the local point-to-point here in Castletowngeoghegan and I liked it. I never wanted to ride in one or anything: I just liked the craic of the whole thing. I never thought I would own a horse but, as time went on and I made a few bob, I eventually bought the farm and started breeding horses, but the problem in this country is that they're generally for sale for flat racing and I've no interest in the flat.

He maintains that, in spite of appearances to the contrary, he really doesn't like any personal publicity and that was ultimately the reason why his horses would run under the banner of Gigginstown House Stud.

> I do an awful lot of stuff for Ryanair and you go along and pull the stupid faces and dress in the stupid costumes but that is PR – you're

trying to promote Ryanair and sell seats on planes. That's all part of the job. Outside of that I don't want – and don't need – either profile or publicity. The reason for the Gigginstown House thing is that I didn't want the horses running under the 'Michael O'Leary' label or the 'Mrs Michael O'Leary' label, or anything like that. This was the only other vehicle I had of not having my name associated with it. Obviously after you win a Gold Cup everyone knows that Gigginstown House Stud is mine, but for a couple of years there nobody knew who or what the hell it was. It keeps my name off the race cards and everything else.

I must have eight or ten trainers now, but I have a terrific advantage in having Eddie to advise me because he knows the trainers who will deal straight with you and you have others who, shall we say, are 'curvy'. Some guys want to train horses and others only want to sell you horses. What you find here in Ireland is an incredible level of talent among jumps trainers and, while they may all have slightly different ways of training horses, ultimately when you look down the list of trainers here, they are all incredibly talented.

In the last ten years or so it has been great, because the best horses are staying here. All my trainers are in Ireland because I like to be in Navan, or wherever, on a pissing wet Saturday in November to see them run. I'd wet myself if any of them get to Cheltenham, but that's only once a year.

Of his start in racing, the Ryanair boss admits he was initially a very cautious owner:

About eight years ago we bought a horse off John O'Byrne called Tuco, which was trained by David Wachman, and he won the Goffs Bumper. It was a most dangerous thing – having a real good experience first time out. He won a few hurdles and we were really minding him to go chasing, but we took him to Punchestown and he fell two from home and killed himself. So I had a very good and a very bad experience all wrapped into one to start off with.

When he killed himself, I'd no more horses because my string consisted of one horse. I decided that would never happen again and I decided I'd have at least fifteen or twenty of them, because you put so much time into minding them and getting them ready that if something goes wrong you've wasted three or four years. I wanted to be in a position where you could afford the odd fatality without wiping out your entire interest. It started from there.

After we lost Tuco, I said to Eddie to go and buy four or five horses straight away. Ger Hourigan had War Of Attrition at the time and was raving about him, but Ger tends to do that anyway. Eddie went out to see him, loved him and we bought him on the day. Eddie had sort of promised Mouse that we'd give him a horse – I hadn't even met Mouse at that stage, it was Eddie who knew him. The idea was that if we were going to have ten or twenty horses in training we wouldn't have them all with the one trainer, because if his yard gets a virus you're goosed. At least if you've a few trainers you've got all the bases covered and that was the plan.

Eddie knew Mouse because he's married to Wendy Hyde and Mouse is very close to the Hydes, so he just knew him of old. Mouse had been at him for about a year that he'd like to train a horse for us and Eddie had told him that when we found the right one, we'd send it to him and see how we got on. We were very lucky because the first one we sent was War Of Attrition. We've sent him a lot of rubbish since, unfortunately, but that's the way it goes.

My earliest memory of Mouse is all about Buck House when he was so successful – the Match race with Dawn Run and all that. He would have come to public prominence at that stage and that's where I first came across the name. He was always one of Ireland's leading trainers – he'd had a few lean years as well – and the great thing about him, as anyone will tell you, is that he is a great trainer of a good horse. He'll mind them 'till the cows come home' and he knows how to train good horses.

That said, he's not the greatest trainer of a bad horse. Some guys are very good with bad horses, getting them handicapped, setting them up and getting a win or two into them. Mouse has no interest in training bad horses, but he is brilliant when you send him the right equipment. There is not a better trainer in the British Isles to train a jumps horse. His record at Cheltenham speaks for itself.

Mouse had a string of maybe forty or fifty horses and, for the last ten or twenty years, that's only been twenty to thirty horses, and yet he has a fantastic record at the Festival. There are others in this country, who shall remain nameless, who have strings of up to a hundred and fifty horses and whose record there is nowhere near as good as it should be. He eats, sleeps and drinks the thing and I'd say that if he could, he'd live inside in the box with the good ones.

To be fair, I'd say he was coming out of one of his fallow periods when War Of Attrition came along. It is well known that he had a lot of personal problems at one point and wasn't training a lot of horses. One's impression was that he was not focused on the training, but I would say that in the last couple of years he'd got his act together and the very fact he was out chasing Eddie to get a horse was an indication that the enthusiasm was back. In fairness to Mouse, he probably would not have got War Of Attrition had he not been chasing Eddie.

A lot of trainers would not be as good as him at training, but they are much better at buying and selling horses and making fortunes for themselves. They sell over-priced horses that are no good to owners who then have a bad experience, get burned and then give up the game. The thing with jump racing is that whatever money you put in, you're going to lose – that's the deal, certainly in jump racing. You do it because you love it and you do it because it's fun and you like the people involved. It is a lot cheaper than buying football clubs.

O'Leary says that at first when the horse went to Mouse the feedback was that this beast could be a serious one, but he maintains that when you own a few horses you expect to get that sort of thing fed back to you quite a lot: 'I now have a few horses with Mouse and I'd send him maybe three a year and generally you'll hear noises that one of them might be something. The thing is that you don't have a clue.'

He recalls that when he and Eddie first got interested in War Of Attrition they were merely looking to expand the string which ran under the Gigginstown House banner and never dreamt the horse would rise to the level he eventually did:

When the horse ran in his point-to-point it was a bit of a joke really. That was one of the reasons Ger Hourigan might have had a problem selling him, because the immediate suspicion is that you have a dodgy jumper. He fell at the last fence in his point-to-point while holding a twenty-length lead. The jockey gave him a haymaker as they came to the last and he over-jumped and crumpled on landing. Even so, we bought him and sent him to Mouse and both he and Conor [O'Dwyer] immediately reckoned that he was a serious animal. 'Serious' at that stage might mean you have a horse that will win a graded race, but you never in your wildest dreams think that you'll win a Gold Cup at Cheltenham or at Punchestown. You know, when you buy five or six horses in any year, that one of them might be good and the rest will be rubbish.

While Conor O'Dwyer would later become inextricably linked with the horse, not least because he was the Gigginstown Stud's retained rider, it was actually David Casey, then stable jockey at Everardsgrange, who initially rode him. O'Leary recalls:

He ran his first Maiden Hurdle at Naas with David on board and was second [behind Zum See], although he performed well. But you're still a bit deflated because this is supposed to be a serious horse. Then we had 'Black Thursday', as I call it. I'd just started dating [wife] Anita at the time and I had three runners at Thurles in November 2003: War Of Attrition in a Maiden Hurdle; a horse called Inexorable, who was a half-brother to Best Mate, and who subsequently won two Grade 3 races and then died jumping his first chase fence in another maiden; and a horse called The Galwayman who was subsequently rated 140 over fences.

Laughing heartily at the memory, O'Leary recalls that he persuaded Anita to come with him to Thurles on the basis that he might have a treble. He was well wide of the mark: 'War Of Attrition slipped on the first circuit and finished mid-division [he was seventh of eighteen runners]; Inexorable was fifth; and The Galwayman finished eighth of fifteen. We still call it 'Black Thursday' and we rarely have any runners at Thurles any more. War had been backed off the board and Mouse was ashen after it – up to eighty Major a minute.'

It got better after that, and quickly, as O'Leary goes on: 'Then he won in Punchestown and he ran in Navan before Christmas where he hosed in, beating Mac's Joy hard held. We were thinking, "Jesus, we might actually have a decent horse here", and thoughts turned to Cheltenham, but Mouse reckoned he'd need one more run for experience.'

Conor O'Dwyer rode the horse for the first time that day and he confesses that he was '… never, ever as impressed with a horse in my life. The way he jumped and the way he went about his business was just sensational. He absolutely bolted in and I hardly had to shake the reins at him to get him going. When I got off the horse, I said to Michael O'Leary and Mouse that if ever David Casey was otherwise engaged, I wanted to ride him.'

While they agreed to this suggestion, Casey was back in the plate next time out but, as the owner recalls, things took a severe downward turn: 'We took him to Naas on the first weekend in January [2004] for a Grade 3 race. He was joint favourite and David Casey was riding and he nearly pulled the horse up, having run plumb last throughout. He scoped rotten afterwards, filthy. So, you're left puzzled really. He starts off poorly, wins two on the bounce and then this happens.'

Despite this setback, the horse was then sent to Cheltenham and, once more, O'Dwyer was booked for the ride. It was, he says, typical of Mouse to allow the horse to take his chance and, on that basis, the jockey was confident that the horse would have a sniff of winning there: 'I thought that if he was at his best, he'd have a shout and I said as much at some of the preview nights beforehand. I knew Mouse would not be sending the horse if he felt it had no chance. I felt that if he was going, he had to be right.'

Michael O'Leary was a little more sceptical and felt that even a top three finish was a mite too ambitious: 'We took him to Cheltenham anyway – despite the bad run at Naas – for the Supreme Novices and he was 33/1 on the day and we thought we had an outside squeak of maybe finishing in the first five. As it was, he ran Brave Inca to a neck to be second and it was a fantastic performance.'

Conor O'Dwyer agrees, even though he says he knew halfway up the Cheltenham hill that he was not going to win:

> He jumped the second last and he must have cleared it by the height of the ceiling. I was looking down on the hurdle from way up. I couldn't believe I had so much horse left but in the end, I suppose, he might just have been lacking a bit in match practice. While he fought his guts out, he was never going to get up to win.

If we'd gone around again, I suspect he'd still have been beaten a neck.

O'Leary says that, on what was only his second ever time going to Cheltenham, the experience of having a relatively successful runner was simply amazing:

That Cheltenham result was great. It was actually only my second time at the venue and it was a real joy to have a runner there and it was an amazing experience. I'm not a punter really, but we had a few bets on him. He was 66/1 on some of the exchanges and I had the odd £100 here and there, lobbing small money on. I'll never forget it: he ran around the outside and at the top of the hill he took the lead and was still there at the second last and I was thinking, 'Jesus, he'll blow up now and he'll be passed', and then by the time they got to the last he was ten lengths clear along with Brave Inca. I then thought he was going to be second, but he kept going and was only just beaten on the line. But we were euphoric, firstly to have a runner there and then to have him placed. You're thinking to yourself, 'Christ it doesn't get any better than this.'

16 War: Triumph and Despair

At this point Michael O'Leary was, he says, in need of a reality check. He simply could not believe it: that he should have a runner at Cheltenham in the first place; and that that runner should finish second in the most prestigious novices' race in these islands. This beast was only the fourth or fifth horse he had ever owned and, while he had had a bit of luck along the way in his career as a racehorse owner, it had never been on the scale he had just witnessed at Prestbury Park. Looking back, he reflects:

He was my first ever Cheltenham runner and he finished second in the Supreme Novices. You're left wondering if it is time to stop. The great thing about something like that is that the dreams will keep you going forever. But you look back at the list of those that have finished second in that race and you see the likes of Best Mate and Kicking King and you start to wonder.

The plan was always that he was going to go chasing. We were only pissing about over hurdles and you're thinking, 'My God, we could have a real chance next year when he goes over fences.' That sort of thing keeps you going all summer long and any time you're having a bad day, you remember that the horse is going back into training soon.

There is great racing in Ireland – throughout the summer with the Galway Festival and then you're into Punchestown and Leopardstown at Christmas and so on, but Cheltenham is something else – just a phenomenal experience, particularly if you're an owner. The first year we went there, there was no pressure on me, but Mouse was white as a sheet and reefing the fags and I couldn't really understand it. The horse was 33/1 and nothing was expected as far as I was concerned. But, in fairness to Mouse and to Conor, they both believed in him. Mouse was telling me in the run up that he was flying at home and doing great pieces of work, but you hear that all the time. I've had two runners in the race since and one was pulled up and the other finished fourth last and both of them had been 'flying' at home beforehand. But Cheltenham is like the Olympics and you have no idea what you have until you go there.

Conor O'Dwyer recalls that in the summer of 2004, following War Of Attrition's Cheltenham debut, his association with the Gigginstown operation became more serious when he went to a friend's wedding in America – that friend being Charlie O'Connor, who works with the Coolmore operation there:

The wedding was on in New York and all the entourage were at it. Myself and Eddie [O'Leary] ended up chatting about the horse and he said that Michael was getting more and more into the racing and he wanted to have a jockey to ride his horses. Mouse had me retained the year before and I said to him that such a deal would suit me, but I'd go home and see what the story was. In the heel of the hunt I stayed with Mouse, but they gave me a retainer to ride their horses when I was available. The following year things were quiet at Mouse's, so they had first call on me. It was all Eddie's doing really and, while Michael knows his horses, he's quite happy to let Eddie sort out that type of detail.

Now that Conor was de facto Gigginstown jockey, his involvement with Mouse's stable star was set in stone and, as the horse embarked on his chasing career, there were very high hopes for his future – hopes which were bolstered greatly by his public debut over fences. O'Leary recalls:

The following year Mouse wanted to run him in a novice chase over two miles, six furlongs, and so he brought him to Thurles – my bête noire of tracks – in November in order to give him experience. Charles Byrnes had a good mare in the race, Sraid Na

Cathrach, and he only just beat her. She was twelve lengths in front at one stage but he won and, fundamentally, the sign of a good horse is one who wins even when he's having one of his off days. Most of my other ones didn't even win on their good days, never mind on an off day.

Conor O'Dwyer remembers that debut vividly:

I thought I was beat at the top of the hill in Thurles that day, because I was niggling him along and I felt that he was a bit rusty first time back. So I sat up on him and gave him a bit of a breather but the next thing, when we turned into the straight, he started to gallop again. He went to the last fence and I'd say I never in my life stood so far off a fence and he must have made three lengths on the leader with that jump and he eventually got up to win by a head. Literally, I never touched him in that race because it was a case that if he was going to win, he was going to win and that was that. From then on we thought, 'Yeah, this fella is the business.'

O'Leary was similarly enthused, although he remembers that the aftermath of that run in Thurles was a little fraught:

He picked up some kind of injury in the van on the way home and he damaged some bones in his back leg and at one stage it looked like he'd be out for the whole season – and if that had been the case we'd have been crushed, because he'd just won his novice chase and it would have been his whole novice chasing season gone. It turned out not to be as bad as we thought, but he was ordered to have box rest for about two months and was confined to his box for that period. He is generally a very good patient though, and a calm horse, so that didn't faze him too much.

So he didn't run at Leopardstown over Christmas, but Mouse ran him at Naas in February and he pissed in that day. With the greatest respect, there wasn't much else in the race and he won hands and heels. But then didn't the fucking hype start: more, I think, because there wasn't much else here in Ireland in the novices' grade. Conor gives an interview saying he thought the horse was very good; Mouse gives an interview saying he's the best horse he's ever had, and it just went on from there. I'm there wishing they'd all shut the fuck up.

On reflection, Mouse also reckons that the enthusiasm they had for the horse got the better of them: 'After he finished second to Brave Inca in the Supreme Novices, the mistake was that I opened my mouth and said that this was one of the best horses I'd ever had. But then the bubble kept bursting every once in a while. We did always think he was a bit special, but we should have said nothing.'

In the heel of the hunt, War Of Attrition ended up as favourite for the Arkle and, as O'Leary says, the closer the race got the worse the pressure became – especially as the horse was regarded as an Irish banker: 'Ireland gets consumed by Cheltenham – all those preview nights and all that stuff. In the end we had a terrible experience. Having gone over the previous year with no expectations, this was terrible. I was talking him down whenever I could, but I was secretly thinking to myself that he could win the thing.'

It was not to be. The horse ran a stinker to finish seventh of nineteen behind Martin Pipe's Contraband. O'Leary rationalises:

> In the end he was simply taken off his feet. It was probably because he didn't have enough mileage up that year. He'd run once in November and once in February, and both times on soft ground. Sure he'd done everything he'd been asked to do, but you generally find that any horse going to Cheltenham with an interrupted preparation does not do the business. The standard there is too high and you'll generally find that the horses who win there have had a good run through the season. It goes that way. He could never go the pace and he was never on the bridle. It was good having Conor on him, because once he realised it was not going to happen, he didn't beat the shit out of him. Conor always minds horses and while he won't spare them in a finish if they have a chance, he won't beat a beaten horse.

O'Dwyer himself reckons the performance was one of the biggest disappointments of his career:

> I remember going to the first and, as the Arkle is, it was an absolute cavalry charge, but while the horse was jumping big, the speed

wasn't there. Sure he's won at Thurles and then at Naas in a common canter, but while we thought that was brilliant, hindsight showed us it wasn't. At the third fence in the Arkle, he ended up out on his nose, lost momentum and confidence as well probably, and that was the end of that. He was very cautious at his fences after that and I just sat up on him. I had as good as pulled him up after the fourth because the race was gone. I could have flogged him to be third or fourth, but for what?

I was gutted because going into the race I felt I was on the biggest ever certainty going to Cheltenham. I came in and said I was sorry and Michael O'Leary wanted to know what I was sorry for. He said that it wasn't my fault the horse hadn't won and in fairness he was brilliant about it. Everyone was as gracious in the losing of the Arkle as they subsequently were about the winning of the Gold Cup, which was brilliant.

Johnny Cummins, whose 21-year career at Everardsgrange was effectively capped by War Of Attrition's ultimate victory in the 2006 Gold Cup, remembers the 2005 tilt at the Arkle at Cheltenham and reckons that the failure to win that race was probably stymied by a rushed preparation:

The year he went there for the Supreme Novices, he'd run previously at Naas and run badly and he scoped dirty after that and it turned out he had a very bad lung infection. It took him a good while to get over that and Mouse did a great job of getting him ready because he took a long time to get right. But Mouse really fancied him on the day at 33/1 and he was only beaten a short head by Brave Inca. He was obviously a real good horse and we hoped that if he jumped a fence that he could be something special.

The next year he cracked a hind splint bone and that meant six weeks standing in. After that, he won at Naas in real deep ground and that probably took more out of him than we realised at the time. He was red-hot favourite for the Arkle but it was probably a rush to get him ready and it never worked out.

The owner says that 'poor old Mouse' was absolutely devastated by the failure in the Arkle, particularly so, as the horse had been so hyped beforehand:

Johnny Francome had been over for Channel 4 before the race and Mouse was on to me as to whether he should let him come and ride the horse. I told him I'd keep the gate closed, but if it meant a bit of PR for Mouse, then than was fine too. So the horse was on the telly and Mouse was interviewed and the hype was huge and then the horse runs no race. I'm just the owner and my business will keep going regardless of whether the horse wins. But when you see the time and effort that the trainer and his staff put into the horses and you realise this is their entire lives. When it works it must be fantastic, but when it doesn't, it's the end of the world.

Mouse always retained faith in the horse, even when he ran inexplicably badly as he did that day. He must have had multiple heart attacks watching that race, but he never lost faith in the horse. He goes though long, dark nights of the soul down there in Fethard, especially when everyone in the business is calling you a useless so-and-so and saying that anyone else would have trained the horse to win.

He called the week after Cheltenham and suggested that we run the horse in the John Smiths Maghull Novices' Chase on the basis that he came out of the Arkle very well and would come on from that run. I said that was fine, as long as he ran at Punchestown a few weeks later.

The horse went to Aintree on Grand National day and, as luck would have it, I am a life-long Manchester City fan and I had organised to take Anita to see them play Liverpool at Eastlands. The only trouble was that it clashed with Aintree. So I didn't get to see the race, but he ran brilliantly to finish second behind Ashley Brook, who had taken off like a scalded cat and had thirty lengths on the field at one point and was never caught. War beat all the other horses who'd beaten him at Cheltenham that day and in many ways he confirmed the promise we knew he had.

We then went to Punchestown for the Swordlestown Chase over two miles and, while we had debated sending him there for the three-mile Ellier Chase, we decided to take on Watson Lake over the shorter trip and he won comfortably. Conor gave him a great ride and, from being ten lengths down coming into the home straight, he jumped past Watson Lake at the last and won handy enough.

All of a sudden we had a Grade 1 Novice Chaser on our hands and, in general terms, horses who do go on to win big things always win a Grade 1 race in their novice year. The question then was what would we aim him for. The Gold Cup didn't seem like a realistic proposition as the Irish generally only seem to win one every ten years or so – Dawn Run, Imperial Call, Kicking King – the trend was there and Kicking King had just won his Gold Cup, so we thought that was not going to happen.

We put him away anyway and he came back here to Gigginstown where he has spent most of his summers, and he had a month off and then a month on the walker before we sent him back to Mouse and back into full training. At that stage Mouse had no real plans for him for his first year out of novice company.

Little did O'Leary – or Mouse, or Conor O'Dwyer, for that matter – know what was in store for them in the coming season.

17 War: The Ultimate Achievement

Conor O'Dwyer firmly believes that every jockey who is lucky enough to win one Gold Cup concedes they are unlikely to win another. He also says that, as the campaign that would see War Of Attrition win the 2006 Gold Cup began, he certainly never entertained any thoughts of adding a second title to the one he had won ten years previously on Imperial Call: 'After I'd won in 1996, I had thought to myself, "Jesus, that's it for me and Gold Cups." I just got on with each race and took it one at a time. I suppose my emotions were tempered by the fact that the Arkle had been such a disappointment when it didn't happen. That sort of calmed everyone down and kept everyone's feet on the ground,' he says. That said, he soon began to notice changes in the horse: 'I could see the improvement each time I went down; you could feel him tightening up and you could feel him coming on.'

The campaign began back at Punchestown towards the end of October where both War Of Attrition and Kicking King were making their seasonal debuts in the *Daily Star* Chase. The reigning Gold Cup champion was the warm-order favourite to win and the connections reckoned that a second-placed finish to Tom Taaffe's charge would be a very respectable outing. It didn't turn out that way, however, as Mouse's horse won confidently by three lengths to provide the first major shock of the season.

He then won Clonmel Oil Chase at Clonmel (after an abortive trip to the James Nicholson Gold Cup at Down Royal which had to be called off following a bomb-scare) and came back to Punchestown for the John Durcan Memorial Chase as a warm-order favourite to pick up the €65,000 first prize. As Michael O'Leary recalls:

I had all the family there and we were expecting great things, despite the fact that his career had shown us that he'd win two or three on the trot before there would be a fuck-up. In the event he ran like a pig and finished fifth, but the worrying thing was that there was no explanation for it. He scoped clean, the bloods were clean, there were no tendon or bone problems – nothing.

Mouse rang me a week later and said he'd found the problem: the horsebox was dirty. There was some problem with the exhaust on the transporter and fumes were getting into the compartments where the horses were. He'd had three horses run that day and they all ran stink. I told him it was probably the fumes from his cigarettes that were the problem and not the exhaust! But at least we had an explanation, even if it ended up posing more questions as to what we'd do next.

Anyway, he was entered in the Lexus at Leopardstown and, frankly, we were only hoping he'd run a decent race. We did not expect to beat course and distance specialist, Beef Or Salmon. In the event it was very soft ground and we'd realised at that stage his best performances were on good ground, so we were not expecting too much. He was well beaten by Beef Or Salmon on the day and coming to the last he was passed by Forget The Past, but stayed on well and reclaimed second. It was good form but nothing earth-shattering.

Of the early season campaign, Conor O'Dwyer says that, while the hype in the papers and specialist media had begun from the moment he beat Kicking King at Punchestown, the connections quickly realised that the ground was going to be a big issue for the horse, because he simply did not act on anything better than decent going. 'He hated winter ground. He couldn't jump out of it and there was no spark out of him at all when he had to run on it. It was quite incredible actually, how different a horse he was on heavier ground as against good ground,' he recalls.

Both owner and trainer are agreed that their options were limited at that stage. They had the choice of taking on the Hennessy at Leopardstown in February – again in all probability in bottomless ground – or going straight to Cheltenham. As it happened, Ryanair were sponsoring the two-and-a-half mile chase at the Festival for the first time and O'Leary was understandably keen for his horse to run in that race but, to keep all bases covered, they ended up entering him for both the Ryanair and the Gold Cup.

For the jockey this presented something of a poser too because, in the pre-Cheltenham frenzy that grips Irish racing fans, preview nights have become de rigueur the length and breadth of the country and, personable man that he is, O'Dwyer is always in demand by organisers. He says:

> It was a nightmare because everywhere you went people wanted to know first off which race he would run in and I was there saying, '*I don't fucking know.*' It was terrible. That got very annoying because the minute you appeared anywhere, you were getting barracked by people wanting to know what the plan was and while I did know what the plan was, I couldn't tell anyone.

The thing was that the owner had one plan while the trainer and jockey had a different one completely. O'Leary maintains:

> In reality the plan was always to run in the Ryanair and while Mouse will tell you different – that the plan was the Gold Cup – the plan was to go to the Ryanair. We were lucky that after his win in the Lexus, Beef Or Salmon was then the hot favourite for the Gold Cup, as debate raged as to whether he could finally put past Cheltenham nightmares behind him. Mick Hourigan is one of the supreme promoters of National Hunt racing and in many ways he can't shut up, which was good for us as it took all the pressure off.
>
> I definitely wanted to run War in the Ryanair, because he was still only seven and you don't want to slit their throats so early in their career – you'd never forgive yourself if something went wrong. But then Kicking King had a tendon injury and other horses started falling out and the picture started changing.
>
> Even so, until the week before Cheltenham we were going in the Ryanair Chase. There was no doubt in *my* mind anyway, partly because I'd been to Cheltenham and had a second place and would give my left testicle to have a winner. I never conceived it would be a Gold Cup – any bloody race would do, the Foxhunter's, anything.

But the week of the race Mouse was still banging on about the Gold Cup and I was telling him: 'Mouse, forget it, you're not going for the Gold Cup, you're going for the Ryanair.' We agreed anyway that if the ground was soft he'd go for the Ryanair, but if it came up good or better he'd take his chance in the Gold Cup. As luck would have it the ground came up good and Conor was happy and Mouse was happy and both thought he should go for the Gold Cup. We had to declare for the Ryanair on the Tuesday, so on Tuesday morning we decided to let him run in the Gold Cup.

The jockey remembers that, in the end, O'Leary left the decision to Mouse and himself:

He literally said to Mouse and myself, 'It's your call'. When he said that, I was going, 'I know what I think, but I'm definitely not going to say it.' Mouse never said it in so many words, but he was never interested in this Ryanair business and there was no way he wanted to run in anything other than the Gold Cup. We were both on the same wavelength in that regard. There was only one race we wanted.

Whatever his views about which race he wanted to run the horse in, the owner was possibly relieved in the end that they plumped for the Gold Cup: 'In a funny way it was almost easier, because he was never going to be favourite for the Gold Cup, whereas if he'd run in the Ryanair he'd have been the raging-hot favourite and you're under all the pressure again with your ass out the window. Anyway, he ran in the Gold Cup and I died and went to heaven.'

★

The 2006 renewal of the Totesport Cheltenham Gold Cup was regarded by many observers as being a wide-open affair. As both Mouse Morris and Michael O'Leary had suspected, all the focus was on Michael Hourigan's Beef Or Salmon, who would ultimately start the 4/1 favourite on a track which had never seen him perform at his best.

Some twenty-two runners took the start for the 3m 2½f contest and, of these, War Of Attrition (15/2), Phillip Hobbs' Monkerhostin (13/2), Michael O'Brien's Forget The Past (9/1) and Francois Doumen's

L'Ami (10/1) were the horses most favoured in the betting ring. Next up was Robert Alner's Kingscliff (12/1), while three others – Willie Mullins' reigning Grand National winner, Hedgehunter, Jonjo O'Neill's Iris's Gift and Paul Nicholls' Cornish Rebel – would all start at 16/1.

But the story of the race was not straightforward, because Mouse had serious concerns: although about six or eight yards of fresh ground had been specially protected for the Gold Cup, the ground to the middle of the course still looked like a 'ploughed field', in his opinion. So it was decided to run War Of Attrition around the inside on the fresh ground (as Best Mate had done when he won the Gold Cup for the second time in 2003). A potentially fatal flaw arose because of the participation in the race of Jonjo O'Neill's talented, but unpredictable, grey, Iris's Gift. A notoriously dodgy jumper over fences, despite having a stayer's hurdle title under his belt, he was certain to go around the inner and could cause War problems.

On the day itself, Mouse recalls that, 'Michael [O'Leary] was very calm and collected, I was far from it.' He also says that while he and O'Dwyer were convinced they had gone down the right road in going straight for the Gold Cup, there were always doubts and he was particularly worried when he saw the state of the ground:

> I walked it in the morning and there was fresh ground on the inner and the outer wasn't too bad either, but the middle was like a ploughed field. It was a disgrace. We had to make a plan there and then and Conor didn't fancy going round the inner too much at the pace they'd be going and, in all likelihood, having Iris's Gift hugging the rail in front of him. But I told him I didn't really care what he did as long as he was comfortable with it and as long as he didn't use the middle of the track. The way I felt was that we were lucky. I mean – Jesus Christ – you have to be very lucky to even get a horse to Cheltenham. Getting them there is one thing and getting them around and in a position to win is entirely another.

Michael O'Leary comments:

> Mouse and Conor had talked it through for days and weeks beforehand and the final instructions were for Conor to settle the horse on the first circuit but then, as they went out into the country

for the second time, to get the horse right into the race. Mouse is convinced that you cannot win a Gold Cup from off the pace – although Kauto Star might have disproved that theory in 2007 – and generally horses that win Gold Cups are in the first four or five as they go out on the second circuit and they are on the bridle, in a rhythm, and jumping well. Also, if they are not in the first three or four at the top of the hill, forget it.

Mouse was spot on as Conor went around the outside. It was a big field that year, because Kicking King was not there and a lot of people fancied their chances. That being the case, around the outside was the perfect way for him to go. If you look at the race again, he jumped like a stag and had a completely uninterrupted passage in what was, in retrospect, a fairly trouble-free renewal of the race.

Keen observer that he is, Charlie Swan reckons that the race was an excellent vindication of the trainer's opinion of his horse:

Mouse always knew he was a good ground horse, but the trouble in Ireland during the season is that you bloody well just don't get it. Invariably you can only run on what you get, but he knew that by the time Cheltenham came around the ground would be drying out and the horse would show his true colours. The horse had actually proven that at Cheltenham, when he was second in the Supreme Novices.

Conor O'Dwyer says that a big race doesn't have quite the same effect on a jockey that it has on a trainer:

Of course you do think about it, but the bottom line is that if you're driving to Thurles for a meeting, the only thing you're thinking about is what you're riding that day. You're not thinking about Cheltenham at all. Closer to the race you focus on it all right, but not for months and months beforehand. I'm sure poor Mouse had a few sleepless nights thinking about it because, for trainers, potential Gold Cup horses don't come along very often. I'm sure it was nerve-wracking for him for months beforehand, but I didn't have the same pressure because I had lots of other things to keep me occupied.

O'Dwyer also remembered an absence of pressure on him before he won on Imperial Call, but that was for different reasons. He says:

> Imperial Call was essentially Charlie's ride and I only got to ride him in the Hennessy because Aidan O'Brien claimed Charlie to ride Life Of A Lord that day. We won that race, but I didn't think any more of it, as I presumed Charlie would ride in the Gold Cup. In any event, Fergie [Sutherland, the horse's enigmatic trainer] rang me three weeks beforehand and said that, with all due respect to Charlie, he wanted me to ride Imperial Call in the Gold Cup. I'm sure he had a big input with the owners, because that's what happened.
>
> Fergie was a great man and he never said too much by way of instructions before a race, but I'll never forget what he said to me before the race that day: 'He's a novice, ride him that way,' was what he told me. I rode him around the outside that day and it worked out brilliantly and it was an amazing day. It had been ten years since Dawn Run had won it for Ireland and there was huge excitement.

Ten years on and the excitement levels were greater still: not only had Kicking King won in 2005, but the expectations of any Irish race-going crowd had reached an all-time high, fuelled by the optimism of the new 'tiger economy'. Greater numbers of Irish winners were now almost *demanded* by the crowd and, by and large, those demands were met.

On the morning of the Gold Cup, Mouse and Conor O'Dwyer oversaw War Of Attrition's last-minute preparations and the jockey says they were very satisfied by the 'little canter around' they asked of the horse. As Conor recalls:

> His lass Noelle took War Of Attrition from us and we walked from the turn-in to the straight, right up to the top of the hill, and we looked at the ground and we both decided that we had two options – run him on the inner or on the outside. The middle ground was pure shite; it was a disgrace actually. That was it and Mouse told me to go home, enjoy the breakfast and he'd see me later. We didn't discuss how we were going to ride him or anything, only that whatever way he was ridden it had to be either on the inside or the outside.

The tensions that build up prior to a race of the status of the Gold Cup are as unnatural as they are unbearable, and each of the connections has their own stresses to cope with. For Mouse, it was the almost intolerable feeling that his personal nirvana was almost within touching distance and he concedes now that his cigarette consumption mounted alarmingly in the hours and minutes before the 'off' as the anxiety levels increased.

For Conor O'Dwyer the pressure was about remaining focused and delivering on the plan he had hatched with the trainer. In the Arkle the previous year, it had all gone pear-shaped and it was now his job to ensure the same thing did not happen again. He did go home and have his breakfast and says that, left to his own thoughts, he felt that a run around the inner was going to be the best policy, because the horse was such a good jumper that this route would not bother him. He says:

> When I got to the races and into the parade ring before the race, Michael never said a word and I think Mouse was waffling on about the weather or something, rather than daring to say a word about the race. There was no chat about tactics and I knew better than to ask. So I just got up on the horse and I went out, did the parade in front of the stands and cantered down to the start. At that point my plan was still to go around on the inner.

It didn't work out that way, however, because at the start, while O'Dwyer was still mulling over his decision to go around on the inside, he asked A. P. McCoy what his plan was aboard the tricky Iris's Gift:

> He said he was going to keep to sixth or seventh place on the rail. I had a change of plan straight away – that was it, I didn't have to think another thing about what I'd do because the one certainty was that I wanted to avoid Iris's Gift. I said to myself, 'The last thing I need is to be behind that grey fucker when he turns upside down.' As it happened he didn't, but I wasn't taking the chance. I rode him around the outside and that was it.

For Michael O'Leary – a man so used to having control of his own and his company's destiny – 17 March 2006 was a different experience altogether. That was a day when he was completely powerless to do anything to ensure his horse delivered the dream. Understandably, though, his clarity of recall remains undimmed:

> He had the run of all runs. Myself and Anita watched it on the big screen near the Parade Ring – the one up over the Tote windows. There is no way of getting out onto the lawn on the front of the stands on Gold Cup day, so it was best to stay where we were. Trevor Hemmings was standing beside us and half the time you didn't know whether to shout or scream, but Trevor's Hedgehunter was running as well and you had to try and keep some sense of decorum.
>
> The last three fences were like this out-of-body experience that I thought was going to be a repetition of the Supreme Novices. At the top of the hill he was in front with Forget The Past, and they went on as they went down into the dip. I'm thinking, 'Jesus, Conor, you've gone too soon', and then they came around the final turn and Hedgehunter and Ruby loomed up and I was thinking, 'Oh shit', but he jumped the second last like a stag and Conor got a few cracks into him. Coming to the last and Hedgehunter was closing, closing, and I remember turning to Anita and saying, 'He's going to fall.' I just had this premonition he was going to fall at the last fence while leading the Gold Cup. He jumped the last brilliantly, but I was thinking, 'He's going to be caught, he's going to be caught, he's going to be caught', before suddenly that changed into, 'Jesus Christ, he's going to win!'

As for his ultimate decision to ride the horse around the outer, O'Dwyer says that some of the rhetoric that emanates from so-called racing experts about the wisdom of riding around the outside annoys him greatly:

> A lot of commentators have a thing about riding on the outer at Cheltenham and most of them have never even ridden a horse. The thing about it is – and what they don't realise – is that Cheltenham is actually a tight enough place because there are so many turns. If you are on the inner and something falls in front of you, if it doesn't bring you down, you're baulked or get stopped completely, and you've to get your momentum going again and it costs you a lot. And, when you consider the pace that these races are run at, it is not

easy to get back the distance you've lost. So, for the bit you give away on the outside, at least you never lose momentum and you can keep going at a nice, steady, even pace. People just don't seem to understand that.

I'd actually watched the Imperial Call video about ten times before I went to Cheltenham with War Of Attrition for the Gold Cup and I'd say that I rode the two horses nearly exactly the same. In fact, on the day they were pretty alike: they were both novicey, but we knew they'd get the trip and they both had a turn of foot.

In the race itself we had a very sweet run throughout and the race really began at the fourth last at the top of the hill and when we started downhill my fella was absolutely cantering. Barry Geraghty was alongside me on Forget The Past and the biggest thing I had to control was my own enthusiasm. I was mad to press the button: I really wanted to go. But I just kept my cool and kept sitting there, knowing that as long as I didn't miss any fence, it would take some horse to beat us. We had to avoid the third last, as it was dolled off because Timmy Murphy had been unseated from Celestial Gold on the first circuit. As we went round that, Barry sort of drifted away from me and as I kicked away from the second last I knew we would not get beat.

He gave me a great leap at the last – absolutely fantastic – and when we hit the ground running I knew we were home and hosed. I knew there was something close at hand, but I didn't know it was Ruby [Walsh] and Hedgehunter. To be honest I didn't care what was there: it didn't bother me because I knew my fella had plenty left. The jump he gave at the last is usually the sort of one you get from a horse halfway through a race when he is full of beans; but, when you get something like that at the last, you know you're going to win. In twenty-five years as a jockey I don't think I've ever sat on a horse who gave me that sort of feeling at the last fence in such a big race. The hairs still stand up on the back of my neck when I think about it.

The collective relief in the War Of Attrition camp as the horse flashed past the winning post two and a half lengths ahead of Hedgehunter was palpable – especially in Michael O'Leary's case:

I couldn't believe it. As the owner you never believe you'll win something like that. Remember, he'd never been over three miles before [and] Hedgehunter will stay all day. And, as an owner, I feel it is always better to win from behind. When you're out in front and everything else is coming at you, you always wonder what will go wrong. But nothing did and the first person I kissed was Anita and the second was Trevor Hemmings. It was a truly incredible experience.

★

Conor O'Dwyer recalls that in the weigh room at Cheltenham there were always a 'few bottles' on ice for the jockeys to enjoy after the final race of the final day of the Festival, but that in recent years the party has become rather more boisterous:

It is a complete madhouse these days. I remember when Imperial Call won the race, I couldn't beg, borrow or steal a bottle of champagne, but when War Of Attrition won, we were practically swimming in it. I'd say we were there that night until about eleven o'clock and we went into town after that. Myself and the wife got something to eat in a Kentucky Fried Chicken shop about midnight; talk about celebrating in style!

The owner, too, had a something of an odd evening and remembers the aftermath as being 'a really strange experience'. As the Gold Cup is on the last day of the Cheltenham Festival, most people are heading home to wherever they came from and thus the O'Learys were left in something of a quandary. Michael O'Leary says:

You don't really know what the hell to do. Do you go back to hotel and tell them you're staying another night and get them to throw open the bar? Well no, because everyone's on the way home. You're scratching around by 5.30pm on the Friday evening. It's a case of, 'Now what do we do?'

As it was, we flew back to Dublin and headed for Mullingar – to the first pub on the way into the town, Moriarty's. We arrived in there around 9.30 with the Gold Cup and nobody could believe it.

By then the first of many celebration parties was already in full swing in Fethard and McCarthy's was packed with revellers, although there was to be a twist in the tail for the winning trainer, as bar-owner Annette McCarthy recalls:

> There had been a real sense of anticipation in the run up to the Gold Cup. I watched it here in the bar and the roar that went up when the horse won was something else. It was like the whole town backed him.
>
> We had a great night afterwards and Mouse actually rang me on his way home and told me to put on a free bar, but I stopped it after a while, because – you know the way – the word had got out and we had a load of fellas in who would never normally be here. But he rang again and when I told him I'd closed the free bar he insisted that I open it again and he said he'd be back here about midnight. When he arrived in he decided he wanted a cigarette – this was in the bar and smoking was banned at that stage – and I said I'd have one too.
>
> Anyway, I pretty much knew everyone in the bar apart from a three or four of them and, as it turned out, when these people were leaving they said to Jasper, my son, that they were going to report us for smoking in the bar. And they did too, but they'd still had a free night at Mouse's expense and they didn't complain about that. It was really annoying and, while in the long run nothing happened about it, you hate it when things like that happen. It took the gloss off the night a bit.

If there were a few sore heads in Fethard the following day, Michael O'Leary was faced with a headache of another sort when he woke up in Gigginstown:

> I got a phone call at around 8.30 the following morning and I was dying. We'd got to bed about 3.30 and when the phone rang my brain was not in gear at all. Anyway, there was this guy wanting to know if we could bring the horse in for the St Patrick's Day parade in Delvin [the nearest village to his home]. I told him that the horse was on the boat home from England, but that I'd gladly bring the Gold Cup along. Anyway what I hadn't realised – and this was

entirely coincidental – was that my racing colours [maroon with a white star] were identical to those of the Delvin GAA club. When we brought the cup into town, there all these young boys and girls wearing the War Of Attrition colours. I couldn't believe it and it was only later I realised the coincidence.

The connections had not yet been able to have a good knees-up together in the same place, so the owner decided to do something about it:

It was a kind of disjointed thing because, while Mouse came back on the plane, he had a car organised to bring him back to Fethard and it was all a bit unsatisfactory. I think if you win a race on the first, second or third day at the meeting, everyone is there and you have a big piss-up and great craic. Anyway I called Mouse the following week and said that we had to have a party. Mouse got Terry McCann in and he transformed the back of Mouse's place with marquees. It was originally supposed to be primarily for the stable staff – Oonagh and Johnny and Noelle and all the rest – but it eventually expanded into something where all Mouse's supporters and owners from over the years came along. It was a great night.

The funny thing about Mouse is that there are very few people who dislike him or get on badly with him and the amount of genuine support and affection for him is amazing. In Ireland there tends to be a lot of begrudgery, especially when someone does well at something. But the level of goodwill for him that night was unbelievable. He'd been through some tough times and people knew that and respected what he'd done. Someone also worked out that it was the first time that a Gold Cup had come to Fethard. They'd had loads of Derbies and Guineas and all that down there, but never a Gold Cup. Apparently, Vincent O'Brien hadn't been based at Ballydoyle when he won all those races at Cheltenham, so Mouse had the honour of bringing the first Gold Cup to the town.

His mother was there that night and his brothers and all his family. You could see Mouse was definitely the rogue of the family. I don't know where Lord and Lady Killanin got him.

For everyone involved with the horse, the victory was only now coming into perspective – as was the fact that this had been yet another fantastic training performance on Mouse's behalf, a feat which Tom Busteed puts into perspective:

> Having a Gold Cup winner is the dream in racing. It is hard, firstly, to get a horse good enough and then to mind him over the years and then actually manage to pull it off. There is a time when you look at the way a horse works and the way he feels, that tells you this is a Gold Cup horse. But saying it is one thing, making it happen is another.
>
> The run up to the Gold Cup in 2006 would have knocked five years off Mouse's life. The tension leading up to that would have been savage for him. He probably doubled his cigarette intake and halved his food intake. He would have given his nerves another shattering and lost a bit more of the hair he's running out of.
>
> Other trainers don't dream of Gold Cups the same way as Mouse does. They're too busy thinking of landing a gamble, or this and that. They don't dream about the ultimate prize because they can't wait that long. Mouse, on the other hand, lives the dream and he's proved that fact.

Demi O'Byrne maintains that with Gold Cup horses, 'the easier the route, the better for the horse', and he says that has been Mouse's philosophy all along. 'We very much saw that with War Of Attrition, where he had the courage of his convictions to stick with the plan for the horse, even though he was beaten by Beef Or Salmon in the last race he ran before the Gold Cup. That's why he's good and that's why he's always been good.'

Further endorsement comes from Tony Mullins, who highlights just some of the pitfalls that trainer and horse had to overcome:

> Mouse was training the horse for a very high-profile owner who had his first Gold Cup horse. Mouse had had a lot of good horses before going through a few lean years and you find in this business that a lot of guys don't come out the other end of something like that. But Mouse is tunnel-visioned about his horses and about

Cheltenham – far more so than any other trainer. I mean, we all love to win in Cheltenham, but you train your horses to win all season as much as you can and then if you get to Cheltenham, well great. Mouse trains solely with Cheltenham in mind and whatever comes beforehand is just a bonus. He's the only trainer I know with that sort of tunnel-vision.

For then head lad, Johnny Cummins, this was not only a victory to cherish for Mouse, but also for all those loyal and faithful staff like himself who had worked with him over the years. It was, he reckons, a high that made up for whatever lows had preceded it:

> Mouse loves Cheltenham and he does things there that he doesn't do anywhere else. The preparations for Cheltenham that year had gone really well and I remember that after one piece of work the horse did, Mouse got very excited. He'd been watching him work from the car at the top of the gallops at home and when they finished he jumped out of the car with sheer exhilaration. But he'd left the handbrake off and the car shot off down the hill. It was a brand new Alfa and it was a write-off.
>
> Personally I fancied him coming up to the Gold Cup and he'd done a really nice piece of work in Gowran two weeks before him. Conor was riding him and we were all impressed, but Mouse kept it all low-key and didn't say a word in the press or anything
>
> My mother, Teresa, was very sick at the time and she died the week after the Gold Cup, so there were mixed emotions for me about the whole thing. She actually saw the race, but died the following week, but I was delighted she was there for him. She was always mad about Mouse and the yard.

Elder brother, Redmond, was actually in Cong, County Mayo, the day before the race with his wife Sheila – an old stomping ground for the Morris family and the location for *The Quiet Man* all those years ago. He says:

> We were at a wedding at Ashford [Castle] the day before with Sheila's mother, Mary, who is one of Mouse's biggest fans. In fact, the day I was first introduced to Sheila's family, I couldn't believe it

when I saw she had a picture of him in her kitchen, so that broke the ice a bit. Anyway, after the wedding we came back to Spiddal and we were on our knees in front of the television screaming the horse home. Every one was so pleased for him because he worked so hard for that.

It was really nice to go to the party down at Mouse's place after the horse won. And what was really nice was that Mum was able to go. She was so, so proud and it was lovely to see her being fêted by all and sundry on the night.

The celebrations surrounding the Gold Cup victory went on for some time in the wake of the race, but even as he was enjoying a sensational return to the front-line of racing fame, Mouse was already plotting War Of Attrition's campaign for the following season and another tilt at the most important race on the calendar. Unfortunately, the fates would not be with him in this endeavour.

18 War: Disaster

Michael O'Leary now admits that while everyone involved with War Of Attrition was ecstatic in the wake of the Gold Cup win, probably thinking they had the next Best Mate on their hands, he was entirely downbeat about the horse's future:

> It is your duty as an owner to be pessimistic and I think I was quoted at the time as saying, 'Well, that's probably it now anyway.' I did so on the basis that most Gold Cup winners never win a second one.
>
> OK, so Best Mate won three in a row, but you have to go back to L'Escargot in 1970 and 1971 to find the next horse to have won more than one on the bounce. Prior to him you had Arkle back in the 1960s. Much and all as I love War Of Attrition, he's no Arkle and, on that basis, I did not actually expect to get him back to Cheltenham. I don't know why I thought that, but I did. Kicking King didn't make it back the previous year, after all, so you'd always wonder.

If there was something prophetic about the owner's feelings – and Mouse being the superstitious type almost certainly feels there was – even he could not have forecast what happened next.

★

The plan for the 2006–7 campaign was going to be roughly similar to what had gone on during his Gold Cup season. A visit to Down Royal for the James Nicholson Gold Cup in November was spoiled only when

Beef Or Salmon scragged him on the line, while trips to Punchestown and Leopardstown for the John Durcan Memorial and the Lexus Chase both saw War Of Attrition struggle in terrible ground conditions. Even so, by now Mouse was saying privately that his stable star was 'a stone better horse' than the previous year and his optimism as Cheltenham 2007 loomed was never more positive.

Then, however, on Friday 2 March 2007, Sheila Morris, better known as Lady Killanin, passed away at St Michael's Hospital in the Dublin suburb of Dun Laoghaire. The news quickly filtered through to Fethard and Mouse immediately contacted close friends to relay the bad news. He was quite distraught at having lost his mother; the two were very close and enjoyed a great relationship. Some might maintain that Lady Killanin indulged her son more than most parents are prepared to do, but Mouse himself is eternally grateful to his mother, not only for realising that he was dyslexic, but also for persuading his father to allow him to abandon school and follow his racing dreams.

Two weeks before War Of Attrition's bid to win a second Gold Cup, this was terrible news but, less than twenty-four hours later, more bad news was to come. Michael O'Leary has vivid memories of the turn of events:

> Mouse rang me on the Friday night to say that his mother was dead and he was in a terrible state. But then he rang me again the following morning and said, 'You're not going to believe this, but the horse has a leg.' Mouse was in a terrible heap; he was devastated by his mother's death, obviously, but he was probably even more devastated by the news of the horse, knowing him. That was that, and my initial scepticism, or pessimism, that War Of Attrition would never get back to Cheltenham was fully vindicated. Personally I was more upset for the horse; I wasn't upset for myself at all.

Conor O'Dwyer has a similar tale to tell, as he got the call on the Friday night telling him Lady Killanin was dead and then the following morning Mouse called again to say the horse was in trouble. He recalls:

> When he told me War was in trouble, my heart nearly fell out of my chest. When I got off the phone I was not sorry for myself that I'd

just lost out on another crack at the Gold Cup, I was sorry for Mouse that all this was happening to him. I was thinking that I'd already won a Gold Cup and that both my parents were alive, while there was poor old Mouse having lost his mother and his idol within twenty-four hours of each other. That thought made it much easier for me to deal with.

Johnny Cummins was actually the person who discovered War Of Attrition's injury and he recalls that the atmosphere at Everardsgrange over that 24-hour period went from one of sustained optimism to one of deep despair:

> Everyone was really gutted. Everything had gone great in the build-up and things were going better than ever and Mouse was more than happy with the horse. He was starting to peak and everything was spot on. I actually fancied him more in 2007 than I did the previous year and, while I know Kauto Star is a real good horse, I really fancied our fellow. But the Saturday week before the race I felt his legs in the morning and I wasn't happy with him and we quickly realised we had a problem. The terrible coincidence was that Mouse's mum died the previous evening.
>
> The horse had a gallop that morning, but when he came back in I felt his legs as I would normally do and there was a bit of heat there and a small swelling. It was just a routine thing that I'd always do, but I didn't like what I saw and we immediately put it in ice, but the swelling didn't go down. The scanner told us the rest: he'd done a tendon.

Typically, when it comes to such a dreadful double scenario as this, Mouse has not got much to say on the matter. He does not dwell on the bad things life throws up; he just gets on with his life: 'It was bad, all right, but what can you do? Obviously the horse was going to be out for a while but, even so, I was determined to give him every chance of getting back to the track and that's what I did.'

Mouse immediately enlisted the assistance of Dr David Chapman-Jones, a medical doctor who, through his company Tendon Works, based near Canterbury in Kent, had pioneered an innovative tendon treatment – clinically established in human medicine – for injured horses.

His most successful equine patient had been Willie Mullins' 2002 Hennessy Gold Cup winner, Be My Royal, who later sustained 93 per cent damage to his superficial digital flexor tendon and was regarded as a horse unlikely ever to be ridden again, let alone raced. However, after ten weeks of treatment at Tendon Works and a total of thirty-five weeks' rehab, he returned to racing and Mullins himself described the treatment as 'quite incredible'.

And so it would also for War Of Attrition, because, by early September 2007, Chapman-Jones was in Everardsgrange to examine the horse. The ten-week treatment in Kent had been successfully completed by early May and he reported himself to be 'more than happy' with the horse's progress: 'He looks much better balanced than he was when I last saw him and he moves so well you'd never think he had a hint of a problem.'

Chapman-Jones professes himself to be 'as sceptical as the next man' of so-called wonder treatments, but he says that his initial analysis of the effect of the treatment on people with chronic Achilles tendon problems showed that 80 per cent of them responded 'significantly positively' to the treatment, in which cellular communication within the tendon is influenced by the application of a very small, cell-specific, sequenced electric current.

According to the doctor, the treatment significantly increases the level of cellular activity that, in turn, increases the level of collagen production and this effectively reduces the level of chronic degeneration – the major cause of injury – and promotes a quicker repair in damaged tendons.

Reflecting back on War Of Attrition's injury, Michael O'Leary says he believes that it is unusual for Gold Cup-class horses to be affected in the way his horse was: 'It is a funny thing that he got a tendon injury. Horses that win Gold Cups are generally so talented they tend to run well within themselves. They tend not to get tendon injuries – something else goes wrong instead. But it is a fair indication of what they go through to win a race of that quality.'

Speaking of how he thought that fateful season might pan out, O'Leary maintains that the plan was to 'mind' the horse – and those were Conor O'Dwyer's instructions every time he ran before the injury occurred. He says:

My basic feeling was that I did not want to lose this horse. I didn't care if he never won again or even ever ran again. We came back after Cheltenham and he ran then at Punchestown, which is tough because a Gold Cup winner is expected to go there and win doing handstands. But he *did* win doing handstands and that was him done for the season.

He will ultimately retire out to my front field and I'd hope we'd have him for a good ten years or so. I would be devastated if anything happened to him in a race and we had to put him down. It is an achievement for the trainer and the jockey if you manage to go back and win a second Gold Cup, but as an owner it is nothing more than an outrageous fluke.

In fact, for me to win a Gold Cup was incredibly, outrageously and unbelievably lucky. Look at someone like J. P. [McManus] who has never won a Gold Cup. I have fantastic admiration for him, but it is incredible, with the quality and number of the horses he buys, that he has not won one. I believe he will win one in time and, OK, so he had one of the horses of the century in Istabraq, but he's not cracked it yet. The thing is that if you're not sanguine about it, you will give up very quickly.

Tony Mullins recalls that the great mare, Dawn Run, was also afflicted by a tendon injury and points out that while it was unbelievable for her to come back, come back she did:

Her injury was slightly different from the one War Of Attrition had, but that doesn't make it any easier to come back from. She showed it could be done, and hopefully Mouse's horse can come back too, but you'd have to say that the odds are against. Mouse knows that too, but I'll tell you, if I had a horse that won a Gold Cup, I'd sleep with him if I thought it would help bring him back. I think that maybe we'll still see War Of Attrition and Kicking King fighting it out at a level just below the top flight. Mouse has the ability and the patience to make it happen and I think that something like that might never happen at a lesser yard, but nothing would surprise you with Mouse.

Frank Berry concurs, saying that a lot of those Gold Cup horses are prone to injury and that Mouse's horse was no different, unfortunately:

> I was involved in the purchase of Jodami for Peter Beaumont and I was convinced he had a few Gold Cups in him, but it didn't turn out that way. For whatever reason, he never did. A lot of jockeys never get to ride in a Gold Cup and a lot of trainers never get one good enough to run in one either. And, even when you do have a good one and they have problems, there is always a younger generation coming along and that's very much been the case with both War Of Attrition and Kicking King. While they've been out, we've had the likes of Kauto Star come along and Denman and that is always the way.

It might have been a disappointment for the trainer who began to believe that the hard-nosed businessman had gone 'soft', but Michael O'Leary's insistence that War Of Attrition would remain out despite the treatment he got from David Chapman-Jones was not something that was up for debate. The bottom line was that the owner had made his decision and was not for changing his mind. O'Leary says:

> They have to get a year off once they have a tendon injury, no matter what you do, be it stem-cell treatment or pin-firing, or whatever. I've said consistently, since he got the injury, it is very difficult for any horse to come back and especially to come back at Grade 1 level.
>
> Having said that, I think the wrong thing to do now would be to retire him; the right thing to do is to take our time. I don't feel there is any point trying to rush him back, so when he does come back, he'll have had a full year off. He'll be ten years old and no matter what the vet says, or what Mouse says, it will be very difficult for him to act again in that sort of company. I'd be loath to do something that would be bad for the horse. But, if there is the slightest hiccup, then that's that. He'll be scanned every time he runs and if there is even the slightest hint of a shadow on the tendon then he is finished. He owes us nothing; he owes me nothing, he owes Mouse nothing. Whatever else I'll be remembered for, I will be a Gold Cup-winning owner and Mouse will be a Gold Cup-winning trainer.

In Ireland at present there are only four Gold Cup-winning owners – three actually, as Mrs Hill is dead – and it is very august territory. The chances of winning another Gold Cup are almost zero. If you are involved in jump racing, having a horse capable of winning a couple of races is a bonus; having one capable of going to Cheltenham and winning there is unlikely, and winning a Gold Cup practically unheard of. Look at Mouse: Buck House was probably his last serious horse before War and that was nearly twenty-five years ago. He's had other good ones since, but that shows you how difficult it is to get a horse capable of winning at Cheltenham – let alone the championship races there.

J. P. [McManus] is still trying to win the Grand National and I believe that if you could sell your soul to the Devil, you'd do it for a Grand National. I don't think you'd do it for a Gold Cup or a Champion Hurdle, despite the great honour and privilege it is to win them. I'd love to win a Grand National, but I know it will never happen. I mean, the race is a handicap, after all. You can win a Gold Cup if you're lucky enough to buy the best horse of his or her generation – and it's the same with the Champion Hurdle. But how the fuck do you manage to find the best well-weighted, handicapping, staying chaser? That is a needle in a haystack. The only way you can win it is to keep throwing numbers at it. Trevor Hemmings finally won it after twenty years of trying, so I suppose that means that J. P. is getting closer every year and no man deserves to win it more.

Reflecting on War Of Attrition's Gold Cup victory and its significance to the trainer, O'Leary maintains that it was 'a vindication for Mouse' and an effective rubber-stamping of his training credentials:

When he started training, he had a lot of success early on and I'm not so sure he actually appreciated that because it came so quickly. When you really appreciate success is when you've had ten or fifteen years toiling away in the desert with shit horses.

But he is more than just a trainer. All right, so he was a good jockey and a great trainer, but he has loads of other interests – he's mad about Galway, he loves Irish music, he's a handy photographer and he's a lot more rounded than many people would think. Even so, he eats, sleeps and drinks horses at the same time.

War Of Attrition was not the making of him in any shape or form, but the horse has brought home to another generation of racing fans just how good he is. He has always operated under the radar in many ways, primarily because he's not one of those trainers with big battalions of horses, and it is harder for the guys like Mouse who operate the smaller outfits to make their mark. Mouse has no interest in the sort of factory operations we see these days. All he wants is forty or fifty good horses that he can campaign well. He also has a good team of people down there and you can tell that they've been with him for a long time. You go to a lot of training establishments and the turnover of people is incredible and you wouldn't know one from the next. There is no agenda [with Mouse] – he just wants to train good horses. A lot of trainers burn their owners; he doesn't.

Speculation and conjecture are racing's two greatest co-conspirators, but we all like to indulge ourselves in this regard and Conor O'Dwyer is no different; he is quite happy to assert that if War Of Attrition had made it to Cheltenham in 2007, he'd have won again:

I would never be cocky about such things, but I felt it was just a matter of turning up, I really did. I thought the only danger would be Kauto Star and I still think we could have beaten him. There was nothing in the race that was ever going to put Kauto under pressure and, in effect, he only had a hold-up horse in Exotic Dancer to beat.

Sitting watching the race, I was thinking to myself when they were about four out that I would have been putting the pressure on and setting sail for home. I don't think he'd have got home ahead of War Of Attrition if my fella was in the same form as when he won the previous year. That's all neither here nor there now, but that's what I think, for what it's worth.

Michael O'Leary reflects that Mouse had a quiet year in 2007, saying that it is probably only natural in the great scheme of all things racing that, when you've won a Gold Cup and a Punchestown Gold Cup, you're probably going to have a quiet year anyway. He goes on:

But he does have a lot of nice young horses coming through and I think he'll do very well in the next few years – as long as he stays injury-free. He has a nice few horses for me and he has a few for Michael O'Flynn. That's what keeps Mouse going – nice young horses coming through, bringing them along the right way and not rushing them. Too many trainers go and blow horses' brains out winning the Champion Bumper in Punchestown. I've no interest in that and neither has he. You bring them along slowly in the hope you might have a decent chaser at the end of it. Mouse will never be Champion Trainer in Ireland, but he is top of the tree. If you have a good horse and you want to get the best out of it, Mouse is your man.

19   Moving On: Venalmar and the Future

It should be no surprise that when War Of Attrition gave notice to the world that Mouse Morris was back with a bang, several familiar owners began to row in behind him once more. Wealthy Cork property developer, Michael O'Flynn, was one of those people and, while his name may not have cropped up much in the story thus far, his involvement with the Everardsgrange yard actually goes back twenty years or more.

Alfie Buller has it that O'Flynn got involved with Mouse as a result of the excellent mare, Mixed Blends: he says that in the second round of horses bought in the wake of Mixed Blends, Michael O'Flynn was one of the shareholders, along with Adam Scott:

> When the Mixed Blends thing went well, we bought five more. There was a new syndicate of five of us and Michael was one of those. The thing is though, that while we all may have lost interest or gone elsewhere in the subsequent years, we all came back again individually later on. I would say that between myself, Adam and Michael we have maybe twenty horses with Mouse now. We all tried different trainers at various times, but at the end of the day we all came back to Mouse. As a man, he would be the first choice of us all, and as a judge, there is something special about him. We only learned that when we went elsewhere.

In fact, between Michael O'Leary, Michael O'Flynn and Adam Scott, by 2007 there was a coterie of horses at Everardsgrange who could be expected to go on to much greater things. This became clear in early 2008, when O'Flynn's Venalmar finished second in Cheltenham and

Michael O'Leary's Hear The Echo won the Irish Grand National, while Adam Scott's Baily Breeze ran into a fine eighth in the Aintree Grand National.

Of those horses, Venalmar was the first up on the final day of the 2008 Cheltenham Festival when he finished a neck second to Willie Mullins' Fiveforthree in the Ballymore Properties Novices' Hurdle, after a race very reminiscent of War Of Attrition's loss to Brave Inca in the Supreme Novices in 2004.

A stunning-looking beast, Venalmar took on a very decent field, including fancied runners such as Nicky Henderson's Aigle D'Or, Paul Nicholl's Breedsbreeze and the main Irish fancy in the betting markets, Tom Cooper's Forpaddytheplasterer. The horse came to the race after starting his career in a Maiden Hurdle at Punchestown in February 2007, in which he finished fourth. In his six subsequent appearances, he was never out of the first two and in his final race before Cheltenham, the Grade 2 Woodlands Park 100 Slaney Novices' Hurdle at Naas in early January 2008, he beat a strong field, including Trafford Lad, who would renew the rivalry at Cheltenham.

The Festival race was delayed for a day in 2008, following the cancellation of Wednesday's racing due to high winds. After enduring an extra day of torture, Mouse was completely ashen and smoking like a peat fire when the horse was finally led into the pre-parade ring at Prestbury Park shortly after 1pm on the final day of the meeting. Michael O'Flynn was there too and, while both men were hopeful rather than confident ahead of the race, O'Flynn confessed that he only hoped the horse would justify the faith Mouse had shown in him since he had arrived in his yard. 'I don't want to win this race for me, I want to win it for Mouse,' he whispered.

In what was initially a slow-paced contest, Venalmar was well up at the head of the field throughout, under new stable jockey, Paddy Flood, and the pair took up the running two out. Over the last he was just leading, but Fiveforthree loomed upsides and, in what was a stirring dash to the finishing line (as a result of which both Flood and Ruby Walsh aboard Fiveforthree were handed bans for excessive use of the whip), it was the Willie Mullins horse that just prevailed, with Trafford Lad four lengths back in third and Forpaddytheplasterer a further length back in fourth.

Mouse was visibly crushed that his horse had not won, but there were no excuses – and for the very good reason that no excuses were necessary. Venalmar had run a cracking race and was just pipped on the line: there was no more to it than that. Discussing the race some weeks later, Mouse was still of the same mind, although he was happy about one aspect of the whole thing:

> I don't think I've ever heard so many good things said by people about a horse that was beaten at Cheltenham. I've always thought the world of this horse and I cannot say that, even in defeat, I've changed my mind any. Lots of people have been very complementary about that run and I'm happy about that and I think he's going to turn into a really good chaser.
>
> I was disappointed he didn't win, but I was not disappointed with the horse. He's crying out for fences now and that's what will happen. Having said all that, though, it was a fair training feat for Willie Mullins to get a horse who'd only run once previously over hurdles to go to Cheltenham and win.

Given his experiences with War Of Attrition, when early predictions about the horse's potential greatness were to dog the trainer, Mouse is keeping schtum about this one. He will allow that he thinks he has a potential good one on his hands, but no more.

For Michael O'Flynn, the whole thing was something of a fairytale. Although his horse did not win the race, he is as aware as Mouse that, barring any unforeseen problems, the horse will show his true colours when sent chasing:

> Mouse is an extraordinary character and there is a lot going on in that head at any given time. And it is all within his head, it is not written down – it's not in files, or on charts or anything, it's all up here [tapping his head].
>
> He's been a friend of mine for many years and it is a friendship I have enjoyed, but I got to know him as a trainer before I got to know him as a friend and, I'd have to say, he's exceptional in both categories. He's the guy that is always in touch and always in tune. The funny thing is that if you looked at him, you'd wonder does he know what day of the week it is.

I'd often drop in to Everardsgrange on my way to Dublin, or whatever, watch the horses on the gallops and then have breakfast in Mouse's kitchen. There is a unique atmosphere there. When you're there helping him cook the rashers of a morning, you realise that everything in that house is done by Mouse. He's a single man these days and he has to do everything himself. But that adds to the uniqueness of the place.

O'Flynn says he loves the way Mouse can plan three months ahead for each of the fifty horses in the yard:

Most people plan day-to-day, but he is able to put a long-term plan together for all the individual horses. I also think he is unique in terms of the relationship he has with all the horses. It is very hard to describe, but I would say Mouse is more tuned-in to horses than most of the people in the business you could ever meet. He has a connection with the horses in terms of what each horse is doing, what a horse is capable of doing, or – even more important – what a horse is not capable of doing. He is very hard on himself in terms of assessment. Some people are always looking at what they did right; Mouse is very hard on himself as to what he did wrong. I would say that the most successful people are those who are hardest on themselves; he's one of them.

Trainers and excuses go hand-in-hand, but with Mouse it is always a case of, 'I fucked up, I used the wrong tactics,' or whatever. We saw that with Venalmar and I find Mouse's assessment to be brutal sometimes, and most often brutal against himself. Seldom does he look for the outside excuse. Some trainers and owners are always pushing to have their horses out there, but Mouse is at the other extreme to that and he will always mind a horse. With him, the horse is paramount and the horse is all that matters – and fuck the owner. He has a way of telling you your horse won't be running, even if you're all prepared to go to Galway, or wherever, with a bunch of friends who are expecting to see your horse running. It just won't happen unless Mouse thinks it should happen.

He laughs when he reveals that, in terms of his assessment of a horse's capability, the one word you don't want to hear from Mouse is 'yak':

That is the key word. If you do hear him describe a horse as a 'yak', or if he tells you the horse is not for you, then that's the time to get rid of it. But if he has something which he likes, the owner is very much part of the whole decision-making process. You know what's going on and you're a central part of the whole experience. He is very much into the relationship between the trainer, the owner and the horse and, quite honestly, there are not too many out there like that.

I have been to lots of places where they have all the bells and whistles, but the atmosphere in Mouse's kitchen, the atmosphere in the yard and the attitude of the staff is completely unique. I love going there and talking to the lads and lasses, but I know trainers who would not like that and would be very possessive. Mouse has no issues like that and, while he is the front man, he respects my wish to speak to people close to the horses, but other than him.

The banter with Mouse is unbelievable; in actual fact, he's a complete pup. Besides the friendship, he is great craic, but people don't see that side to him. I get people saying to me, 'Isn't Mouse fierce quiet, he doesn't talk at all.' But that's not the case at all, at all. You need to know Mouse and you need to be on his wavelength to see that side of him.

I truly believe he deserved what he got in the Gold Cup – nobody deserved it more, and particularly so because horses are his passion. Mouse is only interested in horses; he's no interest in money or material things. Everything he does is about his horses and getting the best out of them. In general, he has very little on his mind apart from his horses. He has no interest in marketing himself or maximising his situation or commercialising his yard. And the thing is that all the people up there with him are the same – the whole focus is on the horses.

As an owner, if you like your horses, then being involved there is a fantastic position to be in, because you know your horses are getting the absolute very best treatment. Some owners will push to have their horses run, but those types wouldn't be suitable to Mouse. There are horses for courses; there are trainers for horses, and trainers for owners. Mouse is a trainer for horses; he's not a trainer for owners. Given that fact, the surprising thing is that he has engendered such loyalty among his owners, because these days so many of them simply want results – and now.

Mouse is a different experience for owners. I mean, last summer I took all my horses home and Mouse was ringing up every couple of days to see how they were. He even came down to Cork to see them! He came down a couple of times! Can you imagine it? It is like a mother rearing her children.

His view is very much that horses are there to be minded so they can fulfil their potential to win races; he's no interest in filling boxes to draw training fees. He could easily have a lot more horses in training, but he's not interested. He is an artist, as distinct from a commercial horse trainer. For most artists it is all about the work and all about what is being created; money is just a bloody awful thing that has to be dealt with.

Cheltenham is not a social event for him, it is serious business. The nervous passion he has in everything he does is unbelievable and I think it separates the good from the great as far as trainers go. Mind you, he could do with a haircut.

There was to be another twist to Mouse's tale before the 2008 season came to a close. That came at Fairyhouse on Monday 24 March when Michael O'Leary's 33/1 outsider, Hear The Echo, ran in the twelve-length winner of the Powers Whiskey Irish Grand National. The performance was a surprise to all the connections – not least O'Leary, whose admission that he had had no bet on his horse sparked 'O'Deary' headlines in the tabloids the following morning.

Mouse himself reckons the result was not the shock some made it out to be, but the preparation for Hear the Echo's run was not the smoothest, as he recalls:

Most of the horses here had been sick since Christmas and most of them were very 'iffy'. Oddly, Venalmar didn't get sick at all, but Hear The Echo most certainly did. But he came right about Cheltenham time and we felt it was worth taking the chance with him. Actually we weren't sure he'd get in to the race, because of the way the weights were working out with Beef Or Salmon top of the weights. We had a small fancy for him all right and Michael was quite happy to run him, so when he did get into the race we decided we'd take the chance.

Four out, and I thought we were going quite well actually [he laughs]. He was jumping magnificently and Paddy is a marvellous horseman. He followed the plan by taking him around the outside, because the horse doesn't like being crammed in too much. He ran a lot keener that we had anticipated and we had more or less decided he'd run out the back, but after about five fences he jumped his way to the front. He was gaining two or three lengths every fence and he was jumping like a buck.

He's not a horse I'd school that much here at home and he has shown a tendency in previous races to make one bad mistake somewhere along the line, but this time round there wasn't a single one. I watched the race with Michael [O'Leary] and I have to say I was thumping the shit out of him all the way. He's probably still black and blue. But it was a real day to remember, especially with Conor [O'Dwyer] announcing his retirement the same day. Conor and myself go back a long way and it was great to see him ride a winner in his last race. All told, it was a very emotional day.

After the horse passed the post O'Leary immediately declared: 'I'm divorcing my wife and I'm going to marry Mouse instead.'

Paddy Flood readily admits that his greatest racing triumph came aboard a horse he did not fancy but he says that Mouse must get the plaudits for having Hear The Echo so right on the day: 'All credit to him. The horse hadn't run since Leopardstown at Christmas, but he had him in the form of his life and I had loads of horse under me throughout the race. He won like a good thing and hopefully he'll go to Aintree for the Grand National next year.'

Michael O'Flynn reckons that O'Leary is a 'lucky fucker' to have won a Gold Cup and an Irish National with horses trained by Mouse. O'Leary readily admits as much, and now, with War Of Attrition on the come-back trail and Hear The Echo intended to run at Aintree next year, he potentially has a lot more to look forward to.

Michael O'Flynn and Mouse himself are feeling pretty lucky too: as well as Venalmar, there are (in Mouse's words) a number of 'fine young horses' at Everardsgrange to keep things ticking over. 'I have small numbers here, but I think the overall quality is decent enough, so things don't look too bad right now. Only time will tell, though,' he says.

It has been a long journey from South Carolina to this point for Mouse Morris – a journey with many ups and downs – but there is certainly a lot more to come from a man for whom the big prizes are the biggest challenge and who has consistently shown he knows how to get the job done. His story still has many miles to run.

Index